'LORD, I need Grace to make it'

Ruth dear: Your ministry in supporting "How Can I Live" means so much: thanks for investing in things of eternal value. II Cor. 4:18

Love, Kay

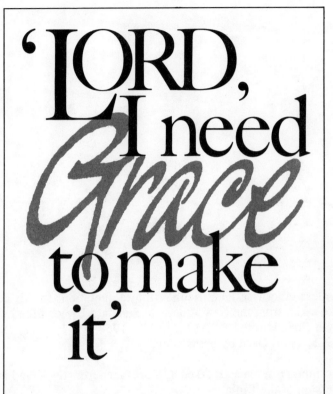

'LORD, I need Grace to make it'

KAY ARTHUR

Unless otherwise identified, Scripture quotations in this book are taken from the New American Standard Bible, ©the Lockman Foundation 1960, 1962, 1963, 1968, 1971, 1972, 1973, 1975, 1977. Used by permission.

Scripture references marked KJV are taken from the King James version of the Bible.

Cover design by Renaissance 2000/Photo by Norhill Photography

©1988, 1989 by Kay Arthur
Published by Precept Ministries
Chattanooga, TN 37422

Printed in the United States of America

CONTENTS

How to
Use this Book

I believe that God in His sovereignty has placed this book in your hand! I believe that this book can be used as His tool for setting you free from misconceptions under which you may have labored for years — trying to be worthy of the grace of God.

If this study is going to be used of God as a tool to free you and ground you in the truth of grace, then you must be willing to get involved in the study by doing the assignments. This work will put you directly into the Word of God. And it is here that God can show you the liberty by which you have been set free so that you do not become entangled again with the yoke of bondage (Galatians 5:1).

This book can also be an avenue of ministry for you as you use its truths to reach out to others and share the liberty of grace.

Whether you are studying on your own or in a group, you will want to obtain our audio or video series which go along with each lesson. You do a week's homework and then have your forty- to sixty-minute discussion (if you are in a group study), and last, either listen to or view the lecture tape. At the end of this book you will find further instructions and a set of discussion questions to assist you with your group discussion.

This book comes to you from a teacher's heart which wants all of the freedom and liberty of God's grace to be yours.

Kay

*For the grace of God has appeared,
bringing salvation to all men.*
Titus 2:11

Grace?
For a Wretch
like Me?

DAY ONE

Could someone who had suffered two mental breakdowns and attempted suicide three times ever hope to be used of God?

Yes, because the **grace** of God has appeared to all men.

But once he had come to know God and to experience the joys of the Spirit-filled life and then had slipped back into the blackness of depression for over a year, could he ever hope to again testify of the sufficiency of Jesus Christ, of a closer walk with Him?

Yes, Beloved, because of that **same grace** that has appeared to all men.

But could a man who had lived a life of atheistic debauchery of the vilest kind — raping women chained in the bowels of his ship, mocking the gospel, and seeking to destroy the simplest shred of faith professed by his fellow sailors — ever hope to know God, let alone be used of Him?

Yes, for the grace of God has appeared to **all** men.

And what if after he had believed in Christ Jesus, he was once again conquered by the lust of his eyes? What if, caught in the snare of flaunted opportunity, he returned for a short time to the raping of women? Could he ever hope to know the power of Christ upon his life, to know the benefits of His mercy?

Or must he live forever in the morass of his wretched failure, condemned to a life of eternal purposelessness because for a short while as a young Christian his life-style reverted to his old patterns? Would the door of hope to a life of usefulness be forever closed?

No, for the grace of God **has appeared** to all men.

The door of hope, the opportunity for eternal usefulness would never be shut. Neither William Cowper, the man who battled depression, nor John Newton, the adulterer, would be denied the sweetness of renewed intimacy with God. The grace of God that would cover all of their sins would also tie them to the moorings of His love and would forever anchor them within the veil of His presence.

William Cowper would write, "There is a fountain filled with blood, drawn from Emmanuel's veins, and sinners plunged beneath that flood, lose all their guilty stains." His heart's cry in his hymn "O' For a Closer Walk with God," would become the heart's melodious plea of generations to follow. Cowper would go on to become one of the major poets of England in the latter half of the eighteenth century!

William's life would touch generations as a result of God's amazing grace which had been bestowed upon him through the testimony of the redeemed slave trader, John Newton. For it was John Newton's story, *Out of the Depths*, that gave William Cowper hope. Cowper was convinced that God's salvation could never reach him. But through the personal friendship of the one who wrote, "Amazing grace how sweet the sound that saved a wretch like me," God would reach William Cowper with His grace. Grace, grace, marvelous grace coming down from the Father above. Amazing grace.

This grace, Beloved, is our subject of study. Grace that enables you to make it . . . no matter your need, no matter the circumstance, no matter the pull of the flesh or its weakness. The Lord is there with His grace, grace sufficient to make it!

Pick up this book day after day for the next nine weeks. Let it take you into the Scriptures. Meditate upon His Word. Do your assignments. Rub in the truths of the Word like oil until it is absorbed into the soul, and you will find it softening the rough, scaly, parched areas of your life that have come from not having enough of the water of the Word.

Everything that I will ask you to do will have a purpose. Don't skip anything. Ask God to open the eyes of your understanding, and then, my friend, you will begin to understand the grace of God which has appeared to all men.

DAY TWO

Have you stumbled and despaired of ever being able to please God? Maybe you failed your God. Maybe you didn't believe what He said. Or maybe you yielded to the desires of your flesh, all the time knowing that what you were about to do was wrong.

Do you weep because you missed your opportunity of service? You made a choice — the wrong one — and now you find yourself imprisoned in the consequences of your own way.

Maybe you have taken account of who you are and what you have to offer, and you are firmly convinced that your life has little, if any, purpose to the Kingdom of God, let alone to the world.

And you constantly wonder, "Why live? Why try? Why keep going when I will never go anywhere anyway?"

Maybe if you were asked, you would check "none of the above." None of these things listed above bothers you. You are settled into your routine Christianity in a routine day-by-day existence. At times it is blah, bland, mundane. But then, considering who you are, "There isn't much more one would expect anyway," you say.

No, there really isn't much more to expect, **except for the grace of God.** As a matter of fact, if it weren't for the grace of God which has appeared to all men, each of "the above" would spell defeat and despair.

O Beloved, if you are going to trust God in all things —
in times of failure,
in times of sin,

in times of weakness,
in times of sickness,
in times of confusion,
in times of distress,
in times of inadequacy,
in times of frustration — then you need to understand and walk in the grace of God which has appeared to **all** men.

For the victorious Christian, the one who lives as more than a conqueror, **grace** is more than a theological term. Grace is a concept of life. It is by grace that one becomes a Christian, and it is also by grace that one lives the Christian life.

Because at one time the Apostle Paul persecuted the Church of God and murdered Christians, he did not consider himself fit to be called an apostle. Yet, it was grace that conquered his feelings, for if anyone understood the grace of God that covers the past and equips for God's future, it was Paul! Listen to his words: "By the grace of God I am what I am, and His grace toward me did not prove vain; but I labored even more than all of them, yet not I, but the grace of God with me" (I Corinthians 15:10). In Paul's writing of those God-breathed words, we see that the whole of our lives is to be lived in the understanding and appropriation of the grace of God. Oh, how I pray that God will grant you this understanding and that He will anoint this writing to your good and His eternal glory.

DAY THREE

The phrase "grace to you and peace" was far more than a familiar salutation often used by Paul in his epistles. In the Roman world where Paul moved, "grace" was a common Greek greeting, while among the Jewish community the greeting was "shalom" (peace). Yet, combined in the context of Christianity, grace and peace took on a whole new dimension of meaning. When the grace of God appeared bringing salvation to all men, it brought with it peace with God to a world alienated from Him by their sin (Titus 2:11-14).

Charis, the Greek word for grace, was a well-known and often-used word which when defined meant "unmerited favor." It was Paul who seized this word from its secular use and developed it in order to describe the unmerited favor which is bestowed upon all those who come to God for salvation through His Son, the Lord Jesus Christ. However, as we study this grace of God which has appeared to all men, we will see that it carries with it an even deeper and richer definition than merely "unmerited favor."

While "grace" appears 213 times in the New Testament, it is used very little in the Old Testament, for there is no single word which fully parallels the New Testament concept of grace. When the Old Testament was translated into Koinē Greek, the Hebrew word *hēn*, which meant "to find favor," was translated as "grace."

In *The International Standard Bible Encyclopaedia* we read, "Much nearer St. Paul's use of *charis* is *rāçōn* . . . 'acceptance.'"[1]

Richards, in his *Expository Dictionary of Bible Words*, suggests that the Hebrew word *hānan* ("to be gracious," "to be merciful") along with *hēn* come closest to the New Testament concept of grace. *Hānan* is used in Psalm 51, a psalm written by David after Nathan confronted him regarding his adulterous relationship with Bathsheba. Although the word "grace" is not readily used in the Old Testament, still we see that even the saints of old understood that God was always to be approached on the basis of grace and never on the basis of merit. The grace of God was seen in His acceptance of a sacrificial animal to cover the sin of man.

Certainly David understood that he had no ground on which to approach God other than God's grace and mercy. Listen to his words in Psalm 51:

Be gracious [*hānan*] to me, O God, according to Thy lovingkindness; according to the greatness of Thy compassion blot out my transgressions. Wash me thoroughly from my iniquity, and cleanse me from my sin. Against Thee, Thee only, I have sinned, and done what is evil in Thy sight, so that Thou art justified when Thou dost speak, and blameless when Thou dost judge. Create in me a clean heart, O God, and renew a steadfast spirit within me (Psalm 51:1-2, 4, 10).

O Beloved, do you understand, as David understood, that God alone can take care of your sin and cleanse your heart? It's all of grace! As you learn to walk in this grace, you will know His incredible peace. Grace and peace to you, my friend.

DAY FOUR

The fact that grace in its fullest sense is not seen in the Old Testament is very interesting to me. I cannot help but think of John 1:17: "For the Law was given through Moses; grace and truth were realized through Jesus Christ." The New Testament is the declaration of the new covenant, the covenant of grace.

Although God has always granted salvation on the basis of grace and grace alone, still grace was not realized until "the Word was made flesh, and dwelt among us, (and we beheld his glory, the glory as of the only begotten of the Father,) full of grace and truth" (John 1:14, KJV).

Until the Seed of Abraham and the Messenger of the new covenant, the Lord Jesus Christ, came, men were "kept in custody under the law, being shut up to the faith which was later to be revealed. Therefore the Law has become our tutor *to lead us* to Christ, that we may be justified by faith. But now that faith has come, we are no longer under a tutor" (Galatians 3:23-25).

It is faith that releases God's grace. Or to put it another way, faith is the key that unlocks the door to the unmerited favor of God. And once that door is unlocked, we forever stand in the grace of God. "Therefore having been justified by faith, we have peace with God through our Lord Jesus Christ, through whom also we have obtained our introduction by faith into this grace in which we stand" (Romans 5:1-2).

What Paul is saying in Romans and Galatians is so vital to a life of peace and victory! I believe that many are living defeated lives because they do not fully realize what it means to live by grace and grace alone. I am not in any way referring to a perversion of grace which would lead to licentiousness, but rather I am speaking of a comprehension of grace which would release the power of God upon their lives, a comprehension which would bring them great peace and put them in the undisturbed eye of the hurricane as they live more and more in the knowledge and experience of the grace of God.

Grace is more than unmerited favor. It is a whole concept of life. It is a concept by which you live, by which you please God, and by which you are freed from religion and released into a relationship with your heavenly Father. Grace is always based on Who He is and what He has done. Grace is never based on who you are apart from Him or on what you can do.

As you think about what has been said, I want you to stop and examine how you relate to your heavenly Father. What is the basis of your relationship with Him?

Have you ever really understood that salvation is all of grace, that there is nothing you can do to merit or earn God's favor? Have you seen that "no good thing dwells within" you which would commend you for adoption as a child of God? What are you trusting for your salvation? And if you are sure that your salvation is all of grace, how then do you relate to God on a day-by-day basis? On the basis of grace, or on the basis of the law?

O Beloved, may we pray for one another that our relationship with our Father would take on new depths through this study.

DAY FIVE

Grace is key to your relationship with God. The believer never comes to God on any basis other than that of grace. Therefore, if you are ever going to understand grace as a concept of life, it is imperative that you understand — really understand — the grace of God which appeared and, in its appearing, brought salvation to all men. I believe that once you have a clear, biblical understanding of the grace and truth which were realized in Jesus Christ through the new covenant, the covenant of grace, that you will have a solid foundation upon which you can construct a life lived totally in the grace of God rather than on whether or not you deserve His blessing, His favor.

O Beloved, I want to pray for you now as I write this and as you, in the sovereignty of God, read it.

O Father, open the eyes of our understanding. Remove the veil of the old covenant so that we might see the glory of the new covenant. I ask this for Your glory and for our peace . . . that it might release us into greater service for You. And I ask it in the name of the Messenger of the new covenant, the Lord Jesus Christ. Amen and amen.

Now let me take you back to the Old Testament, right back to the beginning, to Genesis. Take a moment and read Genesis Chapter 3.

Let me ask you several questions that will be pertinent to our study. Write out the answers by observing carefully what the Word of God has to say. You need not go beyond the Word. Simply get your answers from what you read in Genesis Chapter 3.

1. What did the serpent say that Eve could be like if she would eat of the fruit of the tree of the knowledge of good and evil?

After Eve ate of the forbidden fruit, she then gave it to Adam and he ate. Romans 5:12 tells us, "Therefore, just as through one man sin entered into the world, and death through sin, and so death spread to all men, because all sinned." It was, therefore, at the point of disobedience on the part of Adam and Eve that sin entered into the world.

2. Read Isaiah 53:6 and write it out.

If you and I were to do a study of the definition of sin, we would see that the Word of God says that sin is transgression of God's law (I John 3:4, KJV). Sin is to know to do good and not to do it (James 4:17). It is to act apart from faith, for whatever is not of faith is sin (Romans 14:23). To sin is to come short of the glory of God. Or in other words, sin is to fall short of the image of God (Romans 3:23).

3. After reading what the serpent told Eve she would become if she ate of the fruit of the tree and after reading Isaiah 53:6, what would you say is the essence or the root of all sin?

Because Adam and Eve are the parents of all mankind, all mankind is born in sin. We see this truth expressed by David in Psalm 51:5: "Behold, I was brought forth in iniquity, and in sin my mother conceived me."

You and I are sinners! How can sinners ever hope to redeem themselves when it is their very nature to sin? No one had to teach you to lie, did they? Of course not! Rather, your parents had to encourage you, in one way or another, to tell the truth. Selflessness never comes naturally, does it, my friend? But selfishness does, doesn't it? And is obedience to God natural, or is it a challenge, a battle from childhood on? And the wages of our sin? DEATH! What hope is there for us apart from the favor of God, apart from the gospel of grace? This gospel is first mentioned in Genesis Chapter 3. We will look at it tomorrow.

DAY SIX

Have you ever willfully done something that you wanted to do, knowing full well that you shouldn't? At the time the pleasure of it all might have made it seem worth it. You wanted **your** way, and you got it. But afterwards . . . maybe immediately, maybe years later . . . how did you feel? Can you imagine how awful Adam and Eve felt once they ate of the fruit of the tree of the knowledge of good and evil?

Suddenly they wanted to hide from God rather than have fellowship with Him. Sin immediately affected their relationship, not only with God but also with each other.

Did you notice how Adam and Eve each passed the buck? Adam blamed Eve for what he had done. At the same time, he took a pass at God as he pointed out that it was the woman whom God had given him! In their sinful state, neither of them was willing to confess that their sin was their own doing. That's hard to do, isn't it? It is so much easier to excuse sin in one way or another.

And yet, in the midst of all of this, how did God respond? Did it change the way God would respond? No. God had told them the consequences of their sin before they ever made the choice. Let's take a look at what God had said would be the result of sin so that you will know for certain that the consequences of sin were clearly stated before Adam and Eve were tempted.

1. Look up Genesis 2:8-9, 16-17, and answer the following "W's":
    a. **What** two trees are named in the Garden of Eden?
      1)

      2)

    b. **What** was the clear command of God?

c. **Why** did He give the command?

d. **What** were the consequences of disobedience?

e. **When** would it happen?

2. From your reading of Genesis Chapter 3, did Eve understand God's command? How do you know?

You have seen that Adam and Eve made a choice. The choice was to turn to their own way. They crossed over the line which God had drawn. The line was clearly set as God stated that in the day that they ate from the tree of the knowledge of good and evil they would surely die.

Walking your own way, doing your own thing, being your own god is the root of all sin. You see, God is the One Who is to be pleased. If you choose to be your own god, you are the one who makes the choices, who runs the show, who calls the shots, who is the boss, who is lord or master! And you choose to live in ways which please yourself.

Who is your god?

Adam and Eve thoroughly messed up, and immediately they felt the consequence: death. The day they ate of the forbidden fruit, they crossed over the line of His commandment and violated His standard. God held His line, and they died, in that they were separated from God. The Spirit of God left them, and they were "dead in . . . trespasses and sins" (Ephesians 2:1). Because of sin, they someday would experience physical death. Although God had intended for them to live forever, death had entered the world, and all creation groaned (Romans 8:18-23).

And yet, although the consequence of sin was set, God moved in grace. He did not move the line of His commandment to accommodate man's sin. Rather, holiness held the standard, but God's grace reached over the line to redeem man and bring him back to God. He promised a Redeemer Who would deliver a death blow to Satan, the one to whom they had sold their souls. The first promise of the coming of Jesus Christ, the woman's Seed, is seen in Genesis 3:15. Let's look at it.

Answer the following "W's" which are invaluable when observing the text of God's Word.

1. In Genesis 3:15, **Who** is speaking and to **whom**?

2. **Whom** will the enmity be between?

3. **What** will each of them have?

4. **Who** will bruise **whom** on the head?

5. **Who** will bruise **Whom** on the heel?

6. **Which** is a mortal wound, a bruise to the head or a bruise to the heel?

7. Therefore, of the two, **Who** will be triumphant?

Crucifixion is the only death that bruises the heel. Here is the first promise of the grace of God which would be realized in Jesus Christ! God made an unconditional promise in the face of man's willful disobedience. Grace, grace, amazing grace!

DAY SEVEN

Have you ever looked at things in the natural and said, "No way! There is no human way out"? And there wasn't, short of some sort of divine intervention!

As far as sin was concerned, once Adam had made his choice to follow in Satan's footsteps and exalt himself above God, to be as God, the die was cast. Adam and Eve would reproduce after their own kind. God made Adam "in the likeness of God," but sin distorted that likeness. So Adam became the father of those "in his own likeness, according to his image" (Genesis 5:1, 3).

Redemption by man for man was impossible, for all sinned in Adam, and sinners cannot redeem themselves. Therefore, if God were ever to have man reconciled to Himself, there would have to be a new Adam — a man born without sin, One not born of Adam's seed. The grace of God would have to provide such a One. Jesus would be that man, the Seed of the woman. "But women don't have seeds!" you say. That is right. Normally the seed is given to the woman by the man, and a child is produced.

Are you beginning to see, Beloved, why the virgin birth? In Adam all die because by one man sin entered into the world and death by sin. Connected with Adam's sperm, so to speak, is the gene of sin!

Therefore, one born of man and woman could never redeem mankind, for he would have to die for his own sin. And so God moved in grace. To the woman He promised a Seed Who would eventually triumph over the serpent of old, the devil (Revelation 12:11), by bruising his head. Oh, Satan would first bruise Christ's heel on Calvary. However, the bruising of the heel would not be an eternal wound! Jesus would triumph over death! In the offering of His sinless self, the Just would die for the unjust, and God's holiness would be satisfied. Thus, God would raise Jesus from the dead for our justification (Romans 4:25).

The promise of all of this was not only given to Adam, but it was confirmed to Abraham on the day when Abraham believed God and God, in grace, imputed Abraham's faith as righteousness and made a covenant with him. This account is recorded for us in Genesis Chapter 15. Take a look at it, answer the questions, and mark your Bible so that all of this will stay in your heart. (When you actively participate in a study, you will find that you retain more of what you read.)

1. Read Genesis Chapter 15, and mark each usage of the following three words (and/or their synonyms) in a distinctive way or in a different color. Then, under each word list what you learn from this chapter about that particular word. Ask yourself the "5 W's and an H" (who, what, where, when, why, and how), and see how many of these you can answer about each word you marked in Chapter 15.

      a. offspring, seed, or descendants (Mark these three in the same way.)

      b. believe

      c. covenant

Now I want us to look at one pertinent cross-reference: Galatians 3:16. God wants us to see that once a covenant is made, it is never broken. In this verse Paul explains the relationship of the old covenant to the Abrahamic covenant, which was a covenant of grace. Read Galatians 3:16 and answer the questions that follow.

Now the promises were spoken to Abraham and to his seed. He does not say, "And to seeds," as *referring* to many, but *rather* to one, "And to your seed," that is, Christ (Galatians 3:16).

1. According to this verse, when God promised Abraham a seed in Genesis 15:5 (translated "descendants" in the NASB), Who was that Seed?

2. To be declared righteous is to be saved. How was Abraham saved, by faith or by works? Or to put it another way, by grace or by law?

3. What have you learned this first week in our study of grace, and how can you apply it to your relationship with God?

O Beloved, we have just begun. I cannot tell you what liberty, what peace, what power awaits you if you will but continue in this study. Remember, His power, His grace is perfected in our weakness. You will learn to glory in your weaknesses so that His power might rest upon you! What a contrast this is to what we hear from the world and its reasonings!

Chapter 1, Notes

[1]James Orr, ed., *The International Standard Bible Encyclopaedia.* Vol 2, 1976 reprint. (Grand Rapids, Michigan: Wm. B. Eerdmans Publishing Co., 1939), p. 1292.

*"THIS IS THE COVENANT THAT I WILL
    MAKE WITH THEM
AFTER THOSE DAYS, SAYS THE LORD:
I WILL PUT MY LAWS UPON THEIR HEART,
AND UPON THEIR MIND I WILL WRITE
    THEM, . . .
AND THEIR SINS AND THEIR LAWLESS
    DEEDS
I WILL REMEMBER NO MORE."*
                    Hebrews 10:16-17

Grace?
To Cover
All My Sins?

DAY ONE

John and Charles Wesley knew the Scriptures. As a matter of fact, their lives were devoted to God. In the midst of a corrupt university they had been the instigators of what came to be known as "The Holy Club." Those joining this group lived by strict rules of discipline as they sought to live in accordance with the letter of the law. It was the habit of these brothers to rise at four in the morning for prayer and Scripture reading and to enjoin others to follow their same methods so that they, too, might live holy lives pleasing to God.

Yet, for all their religious exercises, for all their devotion to God, John and Charles Wesley were blind to the grace of God. They had never been "born again." Rather than climbing Mount Calvary and embracing the free grace of God in faith, they agonized to reach the peaks of Mount Sinai, beating their flesh into subjection and wincing from the heat of the blazing fire of the Mount.

Once they climbed Sinai's jagged peaks, they thought they would find Jesus and His peace. Instead of coming into the brilliance of the Son, clouds of darkness and gloom surrounded them. God's voice seemed like a blast of a trumpet. Instead of bringing peace, the sound of His words brought fear and trembling. How well they understood how Moses felt, for the sight of Mount Sinai was "so terrible . . .*that* Moses said, 'I AM FULL OF FEAR and trembling'" (Hebrews 12:18-21).

John Wesley journeyed with James Oglethorpe to America with the intent of converting the Indians, yet he returned to England a defeated, disillusioned man, whipped by the scourge of his own impotence. It was then that he discovered he had been climbing the wrong mountain whereby he had hoped to reach heaven.

John Wesley and his brother, Charles, had totally missed the relationship of the old covenant, the covenant of the law, given at Mount Sinai to the new covenant, the covenant of grace, poured out at Mount Calvary. But they were not alone. They were not the first, nor were they the last, to fail to understand the relationship of these two covenants.

The Pharisees of Jesus's day were so taken with the law that they were unable to recognize the grace of God which was so brilliantly demonstrated in their day. We shake our heads when we read of their blindness . . . and yet, there is a multitude in our day who walk around tapping the same white stick as they grope in the darkness and gloom of Mount Sinai's shadows. They have missed the narrow road of grace which leads to the light of eternal life.

And there are others who have come to Mount Calvary for salvation but who run back to Mount Sinai thinking it is there that they will find the continuing path which will eventually make them acceptable to the One Whom they call Father. And these are most miserable. Although they have been saved by grace, they do not know how to live in that grace.

Beloved, will you pray for those who are living in this state, asking our God to grant them understanding of the grace of God which not only saves but keeps and sanctifies every child of God?

Oh, may we see that the Christian life is **all** of grace. May we ever view Mount Sinai from Mount Calvary.

DAY TWO

Have you ever wondered why the old covenant of law was ever instituted by God if salvation is all of grace and not of law? It is a very legitimate question and one which God is pleased to explain. How I pray that you will be pleased to study it with me.

Some of you may already know the answer. Yet, my friend, I know that as you review this truth God will bless you and prepare you for the other awesome principles of life which will follow in our study. I believe that He will use this truth as a basis for our understanding of our need of grace in order to respond correctly to conviction of sin and to the difficult circumstances of life.

I believe that understanding the purpose of the law will aid you in praying for and winning your loved ones and others to the Lord. Also, you will find the importance of using the principles of the law in the lives of your children until they come to know Jesus Christ.

Four hundred thirty years after God made a covenant with Abraham, promising him the Seed, which was Jesus Christ, God made another covenant. This covenant was the covenant of the law. Galatians 3:15-29 explains the purpose of the law.

Very carefully read this passage which is printed out for you. As you read, remember that grace and faith go together, as do law and works. When you finish, read it again and mark the following words in a distinctive way or in a particular color so that you can readily spot each occurrence of that particular word.
1. seed (and every reference to Jesus Christ)
2. covenant
3. law
4. promise
5. faith

Galatians 3:15-29

15 Brethren, I speak in terms of human relations: even though it is *only* a man's covenant, yet when it has been ratified, no one sets it aside or adds conditions to it.

16 Now the promises were spoken to Abraham and to his seed. He does not say, "And to seeds," as *referring* to

many, but *rather* to one, "And to your seed," that is, Christ.

17 What I am saying is this: the Law, which came four hundred and thirty years later, does not invalidate a covenant previously ratified by God, so as to nullify the promise.

18 For if the inheritance is based on law, it is no longer based on a promise; but God has granted it to Abraham by means of a promise.

19 Why the Law then? It was added because of transgressions, having been ordained through angels by the agency of a mediator, until the seed should come to whom the promise had been made.

20 Now a mediator is not for one *party only*; whereas God is *only* one.

21 Is the Law then contrary to the promises of God? May it never be! For if a law had been given which was able to impart life, then righteousness would indeed have been based on law.

22 But the Scripture has shut up all men under sin, that the promise by faith in Jesus Christ might be given to those who believe.

23 But before faith came, we were kept in custody under the law, being shut up to the faith which was later to be revealed.

24 Therefore the Law has become our tutor *to lead us* to Christ, that we may be justified by faith.

25 But now that faith has come, we are no longer under a tutor.

26 For you are all sons of God through faith in Christ Jesus.

27 For all of you who were baptized into Christ have clothed yourselves with Christ.

28 There is neither Jew nor Greek, there is neither slave nor free man, there is neither male nor female; for you are all one in Christ Jesus.

29 And if you belong to Christ, then you are Abraham's offspring, heirs according to promise.

Now in the space below, list all that you learned from this passage regarding the law. List not only the purpose of the law, but also list what it was never intended to do. To understand this truth is to know how to live in the grace of God on a day-by-day basis.

Let me encourage you to persevere. As we progress, you will see how to live daily in the grace of God in practical ways. I know you want to know how to cope with life immediately, if not sooner. However, my friend, if you are going to live "above it all" — conquering life rather than being conquered by it — you must understand the whys and wherefores of the Word of God. And that will take some time, so be patient. Let's build truth by truth, absorbing each truth as we go.

DAY THREE

Have you ever taken a good look at the Ten Commandments? They really are pretty reasonable, aren't they? No murder, adultery, stealing, coveting. Anyone ought to be willing to keep them, especially if they acknowledge the existence of God. This is exactly what the children of Israel thought.

Then Moses came and recounted to the people all the words of the LORD and all the ordinances; and all the people answered with one voice, and said, "All the words which the LORD has spoken we will do!" And Moses wrote down all the words of the LORD. Then he arose early in the morning, and built an altar at the foot of the mountain with twelve pillars for the twelve tribes of Israel. And he sent young men of the sons of Israel, and they offered burnt offerings and sacrificed young bulls as peace offerings to the LORD. And Moses took half of the blood and put *it* in basins, and the *other* half of the blood he sprinkled on the altar. Then he took the book of the covenant and read *it* in the hearing of the people; and they said, "All that the LORD has spoken we will do, and we will be obedient!" So Moses took the blood and sprinkled *it* on the people, and said, "Behold the blood of the covenant, which the LORD has made with you in accordance with all these words" (Exodus 24:3-8).

From what we have read, it is obvious that the children of Israel found God's commandments not only reasonable, but we see that they intended to keep them. But they didn't keep them, did they?

And what about you? Have you found God's commandments keepable? Have you always loved God? Have you never put anything in His rightful place, thus making an idol of that person or thing? Have you honored your father and mother? Have you ever committed adultery or murder — if not physically, then mentally? Have you ever coveted what another had?

Did you think that you could climb Mount Sinai and raise your hands in triumph as you heard from above,

"Well done. You have kept My law without stumbling in any part of it"?

And when your foot slipped and you found yourself clutching the slippery rock, hanging on for dear life, did you look to the grace of God to rescue you? Or did you pull yourself up, determined to keep on trying to please God?

DAY FOUR

The law was never given with the intention of making a man righteous, whether he was a lost person or a saved person. If you and I could remember this truth, it would forever cast us upon His grace. Grace would become the key that would unlock a life of greater peace, trust, confidence, and intimacy with our heavenly Father and His Son as we walk hand in hand with the Spirit of grace.

Do you remember what you read in Galatians Chapter 3? The law was not given to make us righteous, for then we would not need Jesus Christ and the grace which He brings. Rather, the law was added to the promise given to Abraham — the promise of the coming of the Seed, Jesus Christ, "because of transgressions." (Or it could be translated "for the sake of defining transgressions.") In other words, the law was given in order to show us our sin.

You see, when the children of Israel said that they would keep the law, that all God had commanded they would obey, they didn't take into account, see, or even begin to recognize their inability to keep the law. They did not understand their own impotence to be righteous. The law showed them how a righteous man would live. However, they didn't see their own unrighteousness.

Can you relate? It's hard to see our own inability to be righteous, isn't it? We have a pretty high estimation of man. We think we can do it on our own. If we can't, at least we have to try! Or we have a wrong understanding of God. We think that He won't do what we desperately need Him to do, especially if we don't do our share. We try, at least, to combine our little bit of righteousness and power with His. We think we have to do our part in order to make ourselves a little more acceptable, don't we? I have had to deal with this mentality, and I am sure you probably have also. What do we need to learn to do instead? We need to cast ourselves totally upon the grace of God.

No man, no one, except the Son of Man, ever comes to God for anything on any basis other than grace. Therefore, if we want to walk as more than conquerors, our study is crucial to our day-by-day walk with the Lord because we must live by grace. (If I were you, I'd underline the first part of this paragraph, for it is something you need to remember.)

Think about it, Beloved. When the law exposes sin in your life, what do you do? Where do you turn? How do you respond? Write it out in black and white so that you can take a good look at where you are.

DAY FIVE

On the brink of judgment because they had broken God's covenant and because they had refused to repent, Israel and Judah were given the promise of the new covenant by God. That this new covenant would also be for the Gentiles was a mystery later to be revealed through the Apostle Paul. Therefore, as we look at it point by point, I want you to keep in mind that these promises are for us as well. They are all a part of the grace of God which has now appeared to **all** men.

> "Behold, days are coming," declares the LORD, "when I will make a new covenant with the house of Israel and with the house of Judah, not like the covenant which I made with their fathers in the day I took them by the hand to bring them out of the land of Egypt, My covenant which they broke, although I was a husband to them," declares the LORD. "But this is the covenant which I will make with the house of Israel after those days," declares the LORD, "I will put My law within them, and on their heart I will write it; and I will be their God, and they shall be My people. And they shall not teach again, each man his neighbor and each man his brother, saying, 'Know the LORD,' for they shall all know Me, from the least of them to the greatest of them," declares the LORD, "for I will forgive their iniquity, and their sin I will remember no more" (Jeremiah 31:31-34).

1. From all that you have studied thus far, what was the covenant they broke?

2. How would this new covenant be different from the old covenant as far as the law of God was concerned?

3. According to what you have just read in Jeremiah, list below the other benefits that this new covenant would bring.

4. From reading this passage, Who would bring about all of this — the LORD or the people?

The old covenant, the law, is referred to by the Apostle Paul as a "ministry of death, in letters engraved on stones" (II Corinthians 3:7) and as a "ministry of condemnation" (II Corinthians 3:9). And that, Beloved, is what you will continually live under until you learn to live in the light of the grace of God. It is amazing to me how many Christians do not understand what it is to live in the grace of God, in the "ministry of the Spirit" (II Corinthians 3:8), experiencing God's blessing and help rather than living under a constant feeling of condemnation and impotence.

I am so excited about all that you are learning, and I know that as you learn, you are going to say with Paul that God's grace was not poured out on you in vain but that you labored even more in the furtherance of the Kingdom of God, yet not you, but the grace of God with you (I Corinthians 15:10). I think it is a lack of understanding of the grace of God which keeps many people from living lives that have eternal significance.

That's what you want for your life, isn't it? And yet, do you think, "But I am so ordinary. God could never use me! Look at me! Look at my life! Look at my failures! Look at my inadequacies!"

Stop looking at yourself, Beloved. Look at the grace of God which has appeared to **all** men!

DAY SIX

Have you ever had the fear that you might someday turn your back on the God you love and walk away from Him, denying that you ever knew Him? I have. I knew deep in my heart that it was something that I never wanted to do, but I also understood the weakness of my flesh, the sinfulness of my wicked heart that had so deceived me before.

Or have you ever wondered if God would someday walk away from you, abandoning you, leaving you all alone?

Thoughts like this could keep a person from taking a bold stand for the Lord, couldn't they? We think, "What if God abandons me once I give myself to Him?!" Or we have a tendency to look at our own weaknesses and frailties and think, "I can't, God. Get someone else."

However, once we understand the promises of the new covenant, we can see that all things are possible to him, to her who believes because He will never leave us nor forsake us, so that we can boldly say, "THE LORD IS MY HELPER" (Hebrews 13:5-6).

There is still more in the Old Testament about the new covenant that you need to see so that you will know the whole counsel of God regarding the grace of God. Therefore, let me take you today to Jeremiah 32 and Ezekiel 36.

In Jeremiah 32:38-40, we gain an even deeper understanding of what it means to belong to God, to become His people through the new covenant of grace. Let's take a good look at this passage, for in doing so I know that God will bless you with insight into His keeping power in your life.

You will need to answer some questions so that you see truth for yourself. This process will help you remember these truths! Read the verses from Jeremiah aloud. It will make a difference.

> "And they shall be My people, and I will be their God; and I will give them one heart and one way, that they may fear Me always, for their own good, and for *the good of* their children after them. And I will make an everlasting covenant with them that I will not turn away from them, to do them good; and I will put the fear of Me in their hearts so that they will not turn away from Me" (Jeremiah 32:38-40).

1. As you read these verses, Who is doing the promising?

2. List the specific things God promises in these verses.

3. According to this promise, could you, would you ever turn away from God? Why?

4. How does this compare with what you studied yesterday in Jeremiah 31?

5. For how long is this covenant in effect, and how do you know?

Now let's go to Ezekiel 36:26-27. Read it aloud.

"Moreover, I will give you a new heart and put a new spirit within you; and I will remove the heart of stone from your flesh and give you a heart of flesh. And I will put My Spirit within you and cause you to walk in My statutes, and you will be careful to observe My ordinances."

1. According to this passage, Who makes every provision needed for the covenant?

2. What is done that makes a person different?

3. How does this parallel the verses you looked at in Jeremiah 31 and 32?

4. God's statutes and ordinances are God's law. According to this promise in the new covenant, what are the recipients of this covenant able to do?

Finally, suppose you believed all that you have just read regarding the new covenant, which is realized through faith in Jesus Christ. On the basis of that belief, what have you seen and learned that would enable you to serve God in confidence? How would these truths affect your relationship with God the Father and His Son, the Lord Jesus Christ? Write out your insights below.

DAY SEVEN

The law cannot change a man. It only presents the standards that God requires him to fulfill in order to please Him. And the reason the law cannot change a man is because it cannot transform the heart of a man, a heart which may desire to please God in some way but which can't because it is deceitful and desperately wicked.

At the core of every human heart is self. Peel off all of the layers, layers which may even seem to be good, in and of themselves, and when you come to the core, you will see that all of it grew out of self. Man, if he is ever to be righteous from the inside out, must have a new heart and receive forgiveness for the sins which he has committed.

Forgiveness and a new heart are exactly what the new covenant brings. What man cannot do, God does. The new covenant grants us forgiveness of sins. So glorious is this forgiveness that God remembers the sins no more! Plus, in order to deal with the ever-present problem of slavery to sin, God removes our heart of stone, and He gives us a new heart, a heart of flesh. And not only that, He puts His Spirit within us. Whereas before we were void of the Spirit of God because of our identification with Adam, now, through the new covenant, God in mercy saves us "not on the basis of deeds which we have done in righteousness, but according to His mercy, by the washing of regeneration and renewing by the Holy Spirit, whom He poured out upon us richly through Jesus Christ our Savior" (Titus 3:5-6).

And it is the presence of the indwelling Holy Spirit that enables us to keep God's law, His statutes and ordinances! Thus when we walk by the Spirit, we do not carry out the desires of the flesh (Galatians 5:16). And it is the Spirit within which causes us to fear Him always, and it is the Spirit Who keeps us from turning away from Him.

It is grace, grace, grace. God does it all. Ours is only to believe. And as we will see later, even the faith to believe is of grace! It is all of grace! It is by grace that we are saved. And as we will see, it is by grace that we know Him intimately. It is by grace that we live day by day. By grace we deal with the traumas of life. By grace we serve God. By grace we please God. By grace we deal with our sins when we do not walk by the Spirit but yield to the flesh! It is by grace and grace alone that we can ever approach God and receive the things which we need, whether spiritual, emotional, or physical.

It is through the obedience of faith that we lay hold of the grace of God, believing God and walking through faith in obedience to Him, no matter what.

O Beloved, go to the Lord in prayer. Thank Him for all that is yours through the new covenant.

*And the Law came in that the trans-
gression might increase; but where
sin increased, grace abounded all the
more, that, as sin reigned in death,
even so grace might reign through
righteousness to eternal life through
Jesus Christ our Lord.*
Romans 5:20-21

Grace?
Why Then
the Law?

Day One

John Newton had no excuse for his blasphemous infidelity. From birth to the age of six he had been nurtured on the things of God by his pious mother, Elizabeth. Because her husband was often at sea and she was sick with tuberculosis, many of Elizabeth's days were spent on the couch instructing John in the things of God. At the age of four he could read in any common book. He was carefully taught passages of Scripture, catechisms, hymns, and poems, and when he was six, she began to teach him Latin.

John's father wanted his son to follow him to sea. Yet Elizabeth prayed that John would someday become a preacher of the gospel. God, in His grace and in His time, answered Elizabeth's prayer. But that answer did not come until John had experienced the depths of sin — sin that made him a slave of his raw passions as he rebelled against the knowledge of God.

Elizabeth Newton died when John was six. At eleven he went to sea with his father. It seemed as if his father would have his way, and for a while he did.

When he was but seventeen, John met Polly Catlet, the daughter of the family who had nursed his mother until her death. Although Polly was but thirteen, he fell in love with her. But even John's love for Polly would not keep him from raping at will the black women chained in the hold of the slave ships which he sailed. While he used them for his pleasure, Satan was using John for his. Later he would give testimony, "I rejoiced . . . that I now might be as abandoned as I pleased, without any restraint. . . . I not only sinned with a high hand myself but made it my study to tempt and seduce others upon every occasion."[1]

At the age of twenty-one, returning on a voyage which would take twelve months from Africa to England and to Polly,

> John fouled the ship with his presence. His filthy language shocked even the roughest of the sailors. If any of the crew had a semblance of Christian belief, John sought to shred it. He mocked the gospel and derided Jesus Christ. When in a drunken stupor he nearly plunged overboard into the Atlantic, the ship's captain wondered if maybe John was a Jonah who should be thrown to the whales in order to preserve the lives of the other crew members.

Then one evening as the ship began heading north, John picked up a translation of Thomas a

Kempis' *The Imitation of Christ* and read the words, "Life is of short and uncertain continuance. . . . Today the man is vigorous . . . and tomorrow he is cut down, withered and gone." The words clung to him, no matter how much he tried to shrug them off.

That night a fierce storm struck. John heard the screams of a sailor as he lost his life. "The ship is sinking," voices shouted in the dark. John, along with the others, manned the pumps and plugged the leaks. For hours they labored, seeking to save their lives and salvage what remained of the ship.

Exhausted by his toils and despairing that there was anything else he could do, John muttered, "If this will not do, the Lord have mercy on us." Then he thought about what he had said. It startled him. When he had nowhere else to turn, he had actually acknowledged God and had asked for mercy.[2]

O Beloved, have you ever realized that apart from God, in our flesh there dwells no good thing and that, therefore, there is nowhere else to turn?

Day Two

[The day after the storm] no one else knew what was going on in John's mind. For most of the day he stood at the helm of the ship, exhausted from manning the pumps the night before and steering as best he could. He mused over the question whether such a profane sinner as he could obtain mercy from God. When he tried to recall Scripture verses that spoke of pardon and forgiveness, all that came to his mind were passages that reminded him of judgment. "I waited with fear and impatience to receive my inevitable doom."

Gradually, however, his thoughts turned to Jesus Christ and to the Crucifixion. He recalled that Jesus Christ did not die for his owns sins; Jesus died for the sins of others. The only question that John now had was whether he had gone too far to be included with the "others."

Those eleven hours at the helm were decisive hours for John. Later he wrote, "March 21 is a day to be remembered by me. I have never suffered it to pass wholly unnoticed since the year 1748." He was not yet twenty-three.

As the ship struggled back to England, John began reading the New Testament and was especially heartened by the story of the prodigal son. "The prodigal had never been so exemplified as by myself."

There was no euphoria, no delirious heights of joy as he entered the kingdom. He was still wrestling, trying to understand, trying to see how he fit into God's scheme of mercy. But there was no doubt in his mind that God had hold of him. "I see no reason why the Lord singled me out for mercy . . . unless it was to show, by one astonishing instance, that with him 'nothing is impossible.'"[3]

[John Newton had] wallowed through a muck of experiences in Africa. He had been wracked with disease, had been wasted by near starvation, and had participated in every type of sordid activity imaginable. He had kept a native mistress. Death had seemed commonplace; life had been cheapened; cruelty, brutality, and rape were daily occurrences. And he had gone from the depths of despair and contemplation of suicide to a redeeming relationship with God through Jesus Christ.[4]

O Beloved, what have you wallowed in? Do you think that there is no way out? Do you seem to be caught in the quicksand of sin where struggling only seems to take you deeper in the mire of it all? Grace, only grace can rescue you. Have you seen that? Have you laid hold of it? If not, you will drown in your iniquity. Nothing can pull you out except the grace of God.

DAY THREE

It was the seed of the Word of God that Elizabeth Newton so faithfully sowed in John's heart that God used to bring him to the grace of God. Therefore, I think it is vital that we stop at this point and see just how God uses the law to bring men and women to faith in Jesus Christ.

The clearest and most thorough explanation of the gospel is found in the book of Romans. How I love this book, for it was in grasping a thorough understanding of Romans that I discovered my plumb line for understanding the whole of the New Testament.[5]

In Romans 1:16 through 3:20, Paul establishes the fact that all, both Jews and Gentiles, are under sin. Paul brings his point to a conclusion by showing us the purpose of the law. After having pointed out the purpose of the law, the next point he wants us to see is how God saved us "as a gift by His grace" apart from the law (Romans 3:24).

1. Turn to Romans 3:19-20 in your Bible, and read these verses carefully. Mark them in some way so that they will be

quickly noticed whenever you are looking for these particular verses.

2. Write out Romans 3:20. Read it aloud as you write it. This is another verse you should memorize.

3. According to this verse, what two things do you learn regarding the law?

a.

b.

4. How does this compare with Galatians 3:19?

Stop and think. How was it that you saw your need of a Savior?

DAY FOUR

What can we learn from what we saw yesterday that will help in raising our children and that will help us in our deliverance of the gospel?

As you raise your children, a knowledge of God's law will serve three purposes. **First, the law sets before us the righteous standards of God.** We see what it is to live righteously, in a way that pleases God. ". . . The Law is holy, and the commandment is holy and righteous and good" (Romans 7:12). Therefore, the law shows us what God expects from man.

The problem with the law is not the law; it is us. We are unholy, unrighteous, ungodly sinners. Therefore, try as we may to live according to the law, we will always break it in one way or another. **Thus, we come to the second purpose of the law: by the law is the knowledge of sin.** When we know what God expects and we don't live up to it, we see our sin. As you teach your children the commandments of God and as you explain the commandments so that they can understand them, they will see that they fall short of God's standard. This understanding brings the knowledge of sin. It is sinners who need a Savior. Thus, Jesus came not to call the righteous but sinners to repentance.

It was John Newton's knowledge of the commandments of God and the consequences of his sin that brought him to the grace of God.

The law also serves a third purpose if it is heeded. It serves as a tutor, a schoolmaster to bring us to Christ. Had John Newton listened to his mother and honored all that she stood for and taught him, it would have saved him much grief and remorse. He failed to allow the law to be his schoolmaster.

As you bring your children up under the law of God, you are putting them under a schoolmaster who will not only show them their need for the grace of God, but one who will keep them from the awful consequences of sin (Galatians 3:23-24). The law serves as a guard against a life of blatant sin and the bitter consequences that come from transgressing God's holy commandments.

If only your children would listen to the law, they would not need to worry about the guilt and destructive harvest of immorality, murder, stealing, coveting, etc. Also, there would be no bitterness from broken relationships, for they would honor you and their neighbors. They would not get swept away by witchcraft or the eastern religions, for they would honor God. Of course, try as hard as they might, they never would live perfectly. But they would be kept from the pollution that comes from a blatantly lawless life!

These are vital principles to think on as you raise your children and influence your grandchildren. I believe that the reason so many are suffering over their children is because they have departed from instructing them in the law of the Lord. The parents have neglected the Word of God, and the children have reaped the consequences!

Bring your children up on the law, and keep telling them of the grace of God that can be theirs through Jesus Christ and the new covenant. Pray diligently for them. Then know that you did all that you could do. The rest is up to God . . . and there you must rest. Certainly the lesson seen in John Newton's life is "where sin increased, grace abounded all the more" (Romans 5:20).

Hope in God, Beloved.

DAY FIVE

I believe that many times our witness for Jesus Christ lacks power because we do not allow the law of God to convict sinners of their sin. We forget that Jesus Christ came into the world to save sinners!

Salvation is not merely salvation from hell and eternal condemnation. Hell and eternal condemnation are the consequences of sin. When one is saved, he is saved from sin.

Yet the gospel is often presented as an escape from hell, isn't it? People are told that they need to get saved so that they won't go to hell. It is true that if they are saved, they will never taste eternal death. They will never spend eternity in the lake of fire where the worm dies not and the fire is not quenched. However, the reason that men who have come to the Lord through grace for salvation do not go to hell is because the lake of fire is the consequence of sin.

When a person is saved, he (she) is saved from **sin**. He is freed from sin's penalty, which is eternal condemnation in the lake of fire; from sin's power, which used to reign over him; from sin's presence because he will one day leave this sinful world and go to be with the Father where there is no sin.

Do you see the point I am trying to make? When we present salvation as merely an escape from eternal judgment, we have a tendency to deal lightly with the issue of sin. And when we deal lightly with sin, we weaken the grace of God — the unearned, undeserved, unmerited favor of God — which is poured out on us while we are ungodly, helpless sinners who are enemies of God.

That undeserved, unearned, unmerited favor of God which brings us to salvation is not passive. Grace is active power which delivers us from sin's penalty and sin's reigning power. Therefore, when we deliver the gospel, we need to make certain that we have effectively communicated so that the person sees and understands the following truths:

1. The person must see that he (or she) is a sinner. He must fully realize that he has chosen to walk his own way, to be his own god, and that in the process has violated the holy commandments of God. He must see that he has

known to do good, yet has not done it. He has not walked by faith, listening to, believing, and obeying God's Word. He has transgressed God's law. Here is where the law comes in, for by the law is the knowledge of sin.

2. The person must understand that the just consequence of his sin will be eternal separation from God and eternal condemnation in the lake of fire.

3. The person must understand that Jesus Christ came to save him from his sin (Matthew 1:21; I Timothy 1:15). Jesus did this by becoming a man and by dying in his place as his substitute "that by the grace of God He might taste death for everyone" (Hebrews 2:9).

At this point in our study, I want to restate something to be certain that you haven't missed it: Salvation is salvation from sin; the lake of fire is a consequence of our sin. When our sin is taken care of, we do not experience its consequence. Think about it, my friend.

Will you ask God to lead you to someone with whom you might share all that you are learning, someone who needs the Lord Jesus Christ?

DAY SIX

Let's continue to look at those things which we need to share in order to help people understand the gospel of the grace of our Lord Jesus Christ. There are many who fail to lay hold of the grace of God, yet who think that they are safe as far as eternal salvation. I believe people are in this state because we are not careful to present God's gospel, instead of our version of it. The Holy Spirit convicts of sin, righteousness, and judgment, and **then** He converts. Therefore, as we've seen, we need to be certain to explain that a person is saved from sin, not from hell.

May I urge you to carefully examine what I am saying, and if it is in accord with the whole counsel of God, meditate upon it so that the Lord can give you understanding.

When we deliver the gospel, we need to make sure that people see the following truths in addition to the three we looked at yesterday:

4. The person must see that in love God took his (or her) sins and placed them upon Jesus so that Jesus became sin for him. Because of this, he can have forgiveness of sins and receive His righteousness (II Corinthians 5:21).

5. The person must see that it is necessary to have a change of mind (repent), and he must see that Jesus is God and that He is to be honored as God. This means that he, as a child of God, will be expected to honor God as God rather than being his own god! To acknowledge this is to be willing to be saved from sin. When Adam and Eve chose to disobey God in the garden of Eden, they chose to be like God, to be their own god. Salvation, therefore, reverses this choice. The person coming to salvation is no longer a law unto himself, but he is willing to submit to God and to God's holy commandments. Why? Because salvation does not make us lawless; it makes us righteous.

6. The person must understand that he cannot change his life and make himself righteous. Only God can do this, and He does it by grace through faith. If he will believe on the Lord Jesus Christ, believing that He is Who He says He is, God will do the rest. "For by grace you have been saved through faith; and that not of yourselves, *it is* the gift of God; not as a result of works, that no one should boast. For we are His workmanship, created in Christ Jesus for good works, which God prepared beforehand, that we should walk in them" (Ephesians 2:8-10).

Think on these things until you have a full understanding of them. Then, ask God to give you someone with whom you might share the gospel of grace this week. There is such joy in proclaiming God's gospel. Don't worry about leading the person to Him; that is God's job. Some sow. Others reap. God gives the increase (John 4:37; I Corinthians 3:6-8).

Don't delay in sharing the gospel of His marvelous grace, my friend. "Behold, I say to you, lift up your eyes, and look on the fields, that they are white for harvest. Already he who reaps is receiving wages, and is gathering fruit for life eternal; that he who sows and he who reaps may rejoice together" (John 4:35-36).

DAY SEVEN

I just finished a Teen Conference. I was the last one to leave our premises because from the minute I finished speaking, I had teens lined up waiting to talk with me. Most of them were young men of high school or college age. These teens were convicted of sin, and they were convinced of their need to step out for God.

Once again God has confirmed to me the deep need for those ministering to teens to put away the fun and games and to unsheathe the sword of the Word of God in all of its soul-searching, convicting power.

I've been ministering to teenagers since Jack and I came home from the mission field. As a matter of fact, Precept Ministries began with teens and spread to adults, then to the family. Over the years I have watched teens become more and more calloused towards life. They seem to have lost their fear and respect of adults and of authority in general. Their lives center around themselves and their immediate pleasures. Generally they give little thought to the future, and frankly that is because many of them wonder if they will even have a future. The immediate is what they can see, feel, hear, touch — and they don't want to miss it! So it's "get it now." "Experience it now." And they really think this is okay because they see the rest of the world living this way!

They have been so inoculated by sin that they really don't know how to blush. They have been desensitized to that which is holy and sacred. Much of this desensitization has come from the music, the movies, and the television which continuously bombard their minds. I want to make sure that you know I'm talking only of the majority, not the whole. I personally know there are some godly, serious Christian teens. But for the most part, in the average youth program, they are rare — few and far between.

The God they know is one of love — love as they understand it. It is a love apart from holiness, love that would never hold their feet to the fire so they would walk in obedience, love that would never hold them accountable or make them uncomfortable.

These church kids have heard the gospel over and over and over. They have lit a candle around the fire, walked forward with their friends to receive Jesus, or raised their hands at some youth rally. They'll tell you that they have been saved. And some of them have. Most haven't. They know that God is against sex, drugs, and alcohol, for these are the favorite teen topics at youth groups and rallies. But they don't know very much about the whole counsel of God. "After all, they are teens, aren't they? You can't expect too much out of them, can you?"

The typical, American, church-going teen has been entertained to the hilt. They have been spiritually baby-sat by their youth pastor and his assistants.

What's the problem? Why are so many like this? The problem is that they have never come under good old conviction of sin. They don't understand certain aspects of God's character — His righteousness, holiness, justice, wrath, mercy. They have been spoken at or to, but they have not been taught the whole counsel of the Word of God. They have been entertained but not trained. They have heard about heaven but little about hell. They have been fed philosophy but not been called to the Cross where we are crucified to self . . . and to the world. Everyone else has been blamed for their sorry state. Therefore, they think they are not accountable.

They are horribly deceived.

They desperately need the Word of God delivered without compromise. They need to come under conviction of sin, righteousness, and judgment. They need to have a good dose of the law of God so that they can understand the holiness of God and repent. Tears need to stream down their faces as they experience a godly sorrow which will lead them to repentance. Then they will be ready for the grace of God which has appeared to all men and which will transform them.

That was what happened today. And once again I was convinced that if we are going to effectively minister to teens, then it must be God's way. They must see their sin. Then God can move in His grace, for grace is only for sinners.

Just this past week I received an exciting letter from a young woman we have ministered to through the mail. She sums up what I have been sharing today quite well. Listen to what she wrote:

> After studying the Scriptures and your devotional
> booklet you sent me, I learned what sin actually

is. In the Garden of Eden sin was man wanting to be like God. Sin is man saying, "I don't need you, God. I can be my own God." Sin is independence from God. It wasn't until I defined sin that I was able to see and understand why Jesus must be God, Lord, Master, and Ruler in my life and heart. Before I had asked Jesus to be my personal Savior, but I never surrendered my will and desires and life to Him. I was still occupying the throne. I see now that that was not true repentance, and unless we repent, we cannot have salvation because sin is our saying that we will run the show without God. When we come to Jesus in repentance, we are saying that we can't do things our way, that He must have His way and we are willing to allow Him to be in complete control.

"It is a trustworthy statement, deserving full acceptance, that Christ Jesus came into the world to save sinners" (I Timothy 1:15).

Beloved, use the holy law of God to help men see their sin. Allow conviction to settle in. Don't seek to bypass this crucial work of God. Don't be premature in seeking to relieve people of their misery. Wait and pray. God is "not wishing for any to perish but for all to come to repentance" (II Peter 3:9).

Chapter 3, Notes

[1]William J. Petersen, *Johann Sebastian Bach Had a Wife* (Wheaton, Illinois: Tyndale House Publishers, Inc., 1987), p. 25.

[2]Petersen, pp. 29-30.

[3]Petersen, pp. 30-31.

[4]Petersen, p. 33.

[5]If you have not done our Precept Bible Study course on Romans, I cannot recommend it enough. It will anchor you solidly in the gospel of Jesus Christ.

For by grace you have been saved through faith; and that not of your-selves, it is the gift of God; not as a result of works, that no one should boast.

Ephesians 2:8-9

Grace? But What about My Works?

DAY ONE

Why is it that so many Christians live in defeat, in impotence compared to the power within? I believe that it's because they do not really understand the grace of God which not only brings them to salvation but which also enables them to live as more than conquerors! They do not know how to appropriate grace on a day-by-day basis. Therefore, before we go any further in our study, I want to make sure that we explore the depths of the meaning of grace so that we understand that grace is more than "unmerited favor."

As I have said before, grace is a whole concept of life. To understand grace is to grasp the concept by which we are freed from religion and brought into a relationship with God. It is a concept which not only brings life, but it is also the very concept by which we are to live and to please our Father God. Grace is key to our relationship with God.

The believer never comes to God on any basis other than the basis of grace. I cannot emphasize this truth enough, for what peace, what life, what power, what confidence it would bring to our lives if only we understood this truth and lived accordingly!

Never would you turn away from the blessing of God because you felt you did not deserve it, for those who understand grace know that we are never to come to God on the basis of what we deserve, on the basis of what we have earned, or on the basis of something that we have done that we think has merit. Those who understand the grace of God are ready to appropriate His grace on the basis of faith and faith alone — **faith in the God of grace!**

And never would we stay away from the forgiveness and help of God because we had failed Him in one way or another, for to understand grace is to know that grace covers all of our inadequacies, all of our failure, all of our human frailties . . . and all of our sin.

Rightly understanding grace would also cause us to respect the God of all grace so that we would not seek to cheapen His grace, as some have, by seeking to turn the grace of God into licentiousness. To sin that grace might abound is heresy! To think that we can continue to live in sin because we are under grace is to insult the Spirit of grace (Hebrews 10:29). Living according to the grace of God does not make us lawless! Rather, living under God's grace is to live in ever-increasing holiness.

DAY TWO

Someone has done an acrostic in an attempt to give us a clear definition of the grace of God. Let me give it to you, for it really is very good.

> God's
> Riches
> At
> Christ's
> Expense

The grace of God is everything and anything that you and I will ever need made available to us in and through Christ Jesus our Lord. Grace is God's power at work. And if you really want to understand the grace of God, you need to look at it in its contrasts and its capacity. Let's look at its contrasts first; then, we will look at it in its capacity.

Let's first look at grace in its contrast to debt. A debt is something one owes another and is, therefore, rightly obligated to pay. God is no man's debtor. He does not owe man a thing, for it is man who has transgressed God's law. It is man who is in debt to God. Man owes God a life of perfect righteousness. Yet, that is a debt no man can pay because "THERE IS NONE RIGHTEOUS, NOT EVEN ONE" (Romans 3:10). No matter how hard man tries to pay that debt, he cannot. Therefore, God moves toward man in grace so that although "the wages of sin is death, . . . the free gift of God is eternal life"(Romans 6:23).

God gives man life. God provides life for man, not because He is man's debtor and obligated to do so, but because "the grace of God has appeared, bringing salvation to all men, instructing us to deny ungodliness and worldly desires and to live sensibly, righteously and godly in the present age, looking for the blessed hope and the appearing of the glory of our great God and Savior, Christ Jesus; who gave Himself for us, that He might redeem us from every lawless deed and purify for Himself a people for His own possession, zealous for good deeds" (Titus 2:11-14).

If you read these last verses carefully, you will notice that God is the One Who does the doing, not man! Man is impotent to do anything to please or to help God.

Let me ask you a question. Do you feel as if God owes you something? Do you feel that He is obligated to you in any way at all? If so, why don't you write it down below so that you can take a good look at it? Then, next to what you think God owes you, write out the reason you think He owes you that.

God, You Owe Me   **Because**

Now, how does it look on paper? Do you think God owes you anything on the basis of who you are or what you have done?

Romans 3:24 says that we are "justified freely by his grace through the redemption that is in Christ Jesus" (KJV). **Freely** means "without any cause within ourselves." Therefore, if we are justified — declared righteous when we were sinners — not because of any cause within ourselves, grace is apart from debt. "Now to him that worketh is the reward not reckoned of grace, but of debt" (Romans 4:4, KJV).

Think about it, my friend.

DAY THREE

Have you ever had someone tell you that they thought you were conceited because you claimed to know without a shadow of a doubt that you were going to go to heaven when you died? I have.

Do you know why they thought I was conceited? It was because they thought when a person died that God, in all justice, weighed his good works against his bad, and if the good outweighed the bad, he ended up in heaven! If that were true, Beloved, salvation would not be of grace, but salvation would be of works. Grace and works, as far as being the means of entering into heaven, are incompatible. If salvation is of works, then it is not of faith. It is faith which unlocks the saving grace of our Lord Jesus Christ to us.

We want now to begin to look at the contrast of grace to works. Salvation has always been by grace through faith. Grace and faith go hand in hand and are inseparable. Romans 4:6 says, "God reckons righteousness apart from works"; yet, how many of us really believe this?

I will never forget when after the suicide of my first husband, I tried as a new Christian to witness to my father-in-law. When Tom hung himself, my father-in-law and mother-in-law wanted Tom's death announced on the front page of the newspaper — without any reference to the way in which Tom had died. They wanted all of his achievements listed, and there were many of them because Tom was a top athlete and a top student. His parents were

achievement-oriented. They had made it to the top finan-
cially on their own by their hard work and their cleverness.
We talked about it quite often.

After I had divorced Tom (I was an unbeliever at the
time), I came to know Jesus Christ and was saved by His
grace. I had not seen my in-laws since that time. Several
months after I was saved, in His gentleness God brought
me to the place where I told Him that I would remarry Tom.
It was soon after this time that a phone call came from my
father-in-law telling me that Tom had hung himself. I had
never contacted Tom. I know my father-in-law felt that I
was to blame in part for Tom's death . . . and I was. I had
not been the wife I should have been to Tom. I had not taken
seriously, nor had I properly dealt with, his suicide threats.
I can imagine that my father-in-law wondered who I was to
be telling him about the forgiveness of sins and eternal life
which could be ours through faith in Jesus Christ.

It was a difficult time for all of us, and it is hard for
me to remember exactly what I said to "Dad." I only
remember that he became very loud and adamant with me
as he told me not to worry about him, that he was just fine.
Then, and this I do remember because it so clearly showed
me what he thought was involved in salvation, he told me,
"I am just fine. You don't know how many bricks I bought
for that church. Why, I practically built that church!! I am
a good man."

Nothing I shared convinced my dear "Dad" that his
good works wouldn't get him to heaven. My father-in-law
died several years later. For all I know, I will never see
him again because he did not pursue God's righteousness
"by faith, but as though *it were* by works." He "stumbled
over the stumbling stone," the Lord Jesus Christ
(Romans 9:32). Not knowing about God's righteousness,
and seeking to establish his own, he did not subject himself to the righteousness of God (Romans 10:3).

If salvation is by works, it cannot be of grace. Grace cannot be earned, deserved, or merited, and it is by grace that we are saved through faith (Ephesians 2:8). Grace is seen in contrast to works.

"But to the one who does not work, but believes in Him who justifies the ungodly, his faith is reckoned as righteousness" (Romans 4:5).

We have much to be thankful for as children of God, don't we?!

DAY FOUR

By the time of Jesus, the Old Testament concept of salvation by grace through faith had been eroded by the scribes and the Pharisees. Instead of seeing the law as a means of covering their sin until the inauguration of the new covenant as promised in Jeremiah and Ezekiel, the Jews sought a righteousness through the law. They codified the law, adding to it 613 statutes: 365 negative statutes and 248 positive ones. They felt if they would adhere to these that they would have kept the law, and, thus, God would be obligated to grant them entrance into His Kingdom.

Because they had coded the law, they were certain that they had a righteousness of their own. Thus, when Jesus stepped into public ministry, they were blind to their need of a suffering Savior. They were looking for Messiah, the King Who would give them authority over Rome!

In Paul's epistle to the churches in the region of Galatia, he deals with what he considers "a different gospel; which is *really* not another; only there are some who . . . want to distort the gospel of Christ" (Galatians 1:6-7). How were they distorting the gospel? They were teaching those who had claimed faith in Jesus

Christ that salvation was maintained by keeping the law! They were teaching that believers needed to live by the law. Thus, they were pressing the rite of circumcision.

They did not see the contrast between grace and law. Thus, Paul wrote, "Nevertheless knowing that a man is not justified by the works of the Law but through faith in Christ Jesus, . . . that we may be justified by faith in Christ, and not by the works of the Law; since by the works of the Law shall no flesh be justified" (Galatians 2:16).

My friend, has the veil been removed? Do you really see that there is no way apart from grace that you can be saved, that there is no way you can live in a way pleasing to your God day in and day out except by His grace?

Have you seen the contrast, the antithesis, the black-and-white difference between grace and law? Can you understand Paul's statement that if you are "seeking to be justified by law; you have fallen from grace" (Galatians 5:4)? When Paul made this statement, he was not saying you can lose your salvation and, thus, fall from grace. Rather, he was showing the incompatibility of law and grace. You are justified by one or the other, not both. And if by law, then you are obligated to keep the whole law (Galatians 5:3); otherwise, there is no justification.

O Beloved, there is only one man Who has ever kept the law — the Man, the God-man, Jesus Christ. Why then, having begun the Christian life by the Spirit, do we think we can be perfected by the flesh (Galatians 3:3)?

"If righteousness *comes* through the Law, then Christ died needlessly" (Galatians 2:21).

Think on it.

DAY FIVE

Have you ever felt that you just couldn't come to God and ask for forgiveness again? You should have learned. You shouldn't have sinned again. You wonder how He could bear the sight of you, how He could bear to hear your confession again and again without finally saying, "That's it. That's all. I have had enough. How much do you expect from Me? Don't you know that you are asking too much?"

You are not alone. So many feel that same way. They feel that way because they attribute to God the limited capacity of man. They do not understand the capacity of grace.

Having looked at grace contrasted with debt, works, and the law, I want us to now look at grace and its capacity — its capacity to handle our sin, our failure, our inadequacies.

In Paul's epistle to the Romans under the inspiration of God, we see the clearest explanation of the capacity of grace in all of Scripture. Let's look at Romans 5:12-21.

Romans 5:12-21

12 Therefore, just as through one man sin entered into the

world, and death through sin, and so death spread to

all men, because all sinned —

13 for until the Law sin was in the world; but sin is not

imputed when there is no law.

14 Nevertheless death reigned from Adam until Moses, even over those who had not sinned in the likeness of the offense of Adam, who is a type of Him who was to come.

15 But the free gift is not like the transgression. For if by the transgression of the one the many died, much more did the grace of God and the gift by the grace of the one Man, Jesus Christ, abound to the many.

16 And the gift is not like *that which came* through the one who sinned; for on the one hand the judgment *arose* from one *transgression* resulting in condemnation, but on the other hand the free gift *arose* from many transgressions resulting in justification.

17 For if by the transgression of the one, death reigned through the one, much more those who receive the abundance of grace and of the gift of righteousness will reign in life through the One, Jesus Christ.

18 So then as through one transgression there resulted condemnation to all men, even so through one act of

righteousness there resulted justification of life to all men.

19 For as through the one man's disobedience the many were made sinners, even so through the obedience of the One the many will be made righteous.

20 And the Law came in that the transgression might increase; but where sin increased, grace abounded all the more,

21 that, as sin reigned in death, even so grace might reign through righteousness to eternal life through Jesus Christ our Lord.

1. Now read through the text again, and this time mark every reference to Adam with a stick figure like this ⚲ . Also mark in the same way each pronoun that refers to Adam. Watch for the "one man" which refers to Adam and mark it also.

2. Mark each reference to our Lord Jesus Christ, including the pronouns which refer to Him, and every "One" which refers to Him.

3. Read through the text one more time, and mark the following words in a distinctive way or in one particular color so that you can spot them at a glance.

    a. sin, transgression (Mark these two in the same
       way.)
    b. death
    c. grace
    d. gift
    e. righteousness

4. Finally, list under the appropriate column what you learn about what happened or came through Adam and through Jesus Christ.

Adam   **The Lord Jesus Christ**

Bless you. My heart thrills over your diligence in studying to show yourself approved unto our Lord.

DAY SIX

All of mankind falls under one of two federal heads: the first Adam or the last Adam.

"So also it is written, 'The first MAN, Adam, BECAME A LIVING SOUL.' The last Adam *became* a life-giving spirit. However, the spiritual is not first, but the natural; then the spiritual. The first man is from the earth, earthy; the second man is from heaven. As is the earthy, so also are those who are earthy; and as is the heavenly, so also are those who are heavenly" (I Corinthians 15:45-48).

All of us were born in Adam and, thus, we bear his image. We are born sinners. Adam's single act of disobedience made all who were born of him sinners, and as a result, mankind was condemned!

All of this happened before the law was ever given. Yet, when the law came, man's transgression increased. Why? Because now man knew without a shadow of a doubt what God expected from him, yet man continued to break God's law. Sin abounded.

But when sin abounded, grace did much more abound. God sent another Adam — not one born of the first Adam's seed, but One born of God's seed, born of a virgin. This second, or last, Adam would also be tempted by the devil. Yet, He would not yield to temptation, and, thus, He would not sin.

When Jesus, the last Adam, came, He brought to us the grace of God — grace which would cover not only the first Adam's sin, but the sins of all mankind! Jesus's one act of righteousness would make available to all men justification and life so that Jesus, the last Adam, could restore to mankind what man had lost in the first Adam.

The capacity of grace would cover the sins of all mankind from the time of Adam to the coming of the Son of Man in great glory and power so that no matter how great our sins, how weak our flesh, how often we failed, there would be grace abounding. Never would there be a thing that we could do or fail to do that could not be covered by the grace of God.

But you may say to me, "Kay, you do not know what I have done! You don't know how weak I am. You don't know how often I have failed. How can God forgive me, accept me again, restore me, use me?"

It is grace, Beloved! Not cheap grace, but grace that cost a very great price. Grace that caused the death of Jesus Christ, the innocent for the guilty. Grace that banishes condemnation and brings justification. Grace that covers the inadequacies, the failures, and the sins of the justified for the remainder of their days on earth. Grace that can do all that and whatever else you need — because of its great capacity!

Do you live in defeat and spiritual impotence because you are ignorant of the abounding grace of God? Stop, my friend. Don't let His grace be poured out on you in vain.

DAY SEVEN

Brownlow North was a ladies' man — handsome, rich, smooth on the dance floor, brilliant astride a horse. It was easy to propose to nineteen young women one after another, all adoringly consenting to this young man who swept them off their feet.

Although raised by a godly mother who not only taught him the truths of Jesus Christ but earnestly prayed for him, Brownlow drank heavily and gambled constantly. Then at the age of thirty-three, it seemed for a while that his mother's prayers had finally been answered by God. After the near death of his son, Brownlow became conscious of his sins and went to Oxford, England, where he decided he would "read for holy orders." He was set on becoming a clergyman in the Church of England until the Bishop became aware of Brownlow's past. When ordination was denied him, in disappointment he returned not only to his gambling and drinking, but he took up mocking anything that was righteous. He was not prepared to live righteously again.

Then at the age of forty-four, he was suddenly attacked with pains which racked his body with such violence that he was sure he was going to die.

> Dropping his cigar he gasped to his son, 'I am a dead man, take me upstairs.' They helped him to his room and he threw himself on his bed. 'My first thought then was, "Now, what will my forty-four years of following the devices of my own heart profit me? In a few minutes I shall be in hell." At that moment I felt constrained to pray, but it was merely the prayer of a coward, a cry for mercy. I was not sorry for what I had done, but I was afraid of the punishment of my sin.'

> The housemaid hurried in to light the fire, while her master lay groaning on the bed. Unwittingly, she had a part to play in that night's work. 'Though I did not believe it at that time,' continues North's account, 'that I had ten minutes to live, and knew that there was no possible hope for me but in the mercy of God, and that if I did not seek that mercy I could not expect to have it, yet such was the nature of my heart that it was a balance with me, a thing to turn this way or that, I could not tell how, whether I should wait till that woman left the room or whether I should fall on my knees and cry for mercy in her presence.'

> The girl struck a match, and the fire blazed up. At that moment she heard a movement behind her and turned round. To her astonishment her pagan master was on his knees — and praying aloud. 'I believe it was a turning point with me,' said North in after years. 'I believe that if I had at that time resisted the Holy Ghost it would have been once too often.'

The next day he told his guests that he had given his heart to Christ. 'He seemed as if just risen from a long illness, and very gentle and subdued in manner.' Family prayers were instituted forthwith, and his dissolute friends informed that 'I am, I trust by the grace of God, a changed man.' His aged mother, when he went to see her, said, 'Brownlow, God is not only able to save you but to make you more conspicuous for good than ever you were for evil.'

The past now caught up with him. Weary weeks and months of spiritual conflict assailed him. Temptations, doubts as to his salvation, the suspicion of those who might have helped but doubted his sincerity, cravings for the alcohol which he had abjured, all this put him through the fire. He read nothing but the Bible. His wife would hear him groaning aloud and find him rolling on the carpet, agonising in prayer. He would listen greedily to the exposition of Scripture. . . .

One preacher said, "He looks as if he had been a servant of evil and yet he looks as if yielding wholly to God."

At last, after six months of stress North realised, late one night when he could not sleep and had turned back to his Bible and was studying Romans, that Christ had done all that was needed, that a simple trust in Him was sufficient for life and death.

Months later Brownlow North, quite by accident, found himself filling pulpits in Scotland. He became Scotland's most popular lay preacher, filling churches, making the most unlikely men and women concerned about their souls and bringing them to Christ. The public astonishment was great. Newspapers suggested it was done for a wager.

One night, as North was about to enter the pulpit in a highland town, a man handed him a letter, asking him to read it before he preached. The letter reminded him in no uncertain terms of some of the more repulsive excesses of his past and ended, 'How dare you pray and speak to the people this evening when you are such a vile sinner?' North mounted the pulpit and the service began. At sermon time he announced his text, looked down at the sea of expectant faces — and read out the letter. The hush was intense. He spoke again: 'All that is here said is true. It is a correct picture of the degraded sinner I once was. And oh — how wonderful must the grace be that could raise me up from such a death in trespasses and sins and make me what I appear before you to-night, a vessel of mercy, one who knows that all his past sins have been cleansed away through the atoning blood of the Lamb of God. It is of His redeeming love that I now have to tell you. . .'

'I'll tell you what I am,' he would say, 'I am a man who has been at the brink of the bottomless pit and has looked in, and as I see many of you going down to that pit I am here to "hollo" you back, and warn you of your danger. I am here as the chief of sinners, saved by grace, to tell you that the grace which has saved me can surely save you.'[1]

O Beloved, have you seen the great capacity of the grace of God? Have you drawn all that you need from its all-sufficient well with your bucket of faith?

What is keeping you from appropriating what God has so freely given you? Write it out below. Then, consider it in the light of what you have already seen and in the light of what you will see in the days to come.

"GOD . . . GIVES GRACE TO THE HUMBLE" (James 4:6).

Chapter 4, Notes

[1]John Pollock, *A Fistful of Heroes* (Hants, UK: Marshall Pickering, 1988), pp. 87-90.

And He has said to me, "My grace is sufficient for you, for power is perfected in weakness." Most gladly, therefore, I will rather boast about my weaknesses, that the power of Christ may dwell in me. Therefore I am well content with weaknesses, with insults, with distresses, with persecutions, with difficulties, for Christ's sake; for when I am weak, then I am strong.

II Corinthians 12:9-10

Grace?
Sufficient
for Every Day?

DAY ONE

Truly John Newton's salvation was all of God's grace, yet John had still another lesson to learn regarding the grace of God. And so do we, my friend.

John knew what it was to be saved by grace through faith from the penalty of sin. Now, in a very painful way he was to learn a lesson on grace that he would never forget. Grace not only delivers us from sin's penalty, but it is also by grace that we are saved through faith from the power of sin.

After John saw Polly and she gave her consent for him to pursue their relationship, he was back off on another slave run to Africa.

John felt things were under control. He felt reasonably good about life. Romantically he was communicating with Polly, and spiritually he was in touch with God. Vocationally he was first mate on a slave ship and had been promised the opportunity of becoming a sea captain his next time out. What more could a young Christian ask? For a young man of twenty-three, who as yet had no compunctions against slavery, the future looked promising.

But the rosy outlook lasted only a few weeks. By the time the ship landed on Africa's west coast, as John puts it, "I was almost as bad as before." He had stopped reading his Bible, had become careless in prayer, and had no Christian fellowship. "The enemy prepared a train of temptations and I became his easy prey. For about a month, he lulled me asleep in a course of evil, of which a few months before, I could not have supposed myself any longer capable."

. . . In the hold of the ship were naked slave girls. It was customary for the officers to have their pick. Momentarily he pushed away the temptation, but then, "I was now fast bound in chains; I had little desire and no power to free myself." So he descended into the hold, picked out a girl, and raped her.

Off the boat he was provided "a black girl for his pleasure." His life-style reverted to his old patterns. "If I attempted to struggle, it was in vain."

Then illness struck. He was reminded of his previous illness in Sierra Leone and the depths into which he had sunk at that time. Would this be the pattern again?

At first he despaired of finding divine forgiveness; the "door of hope" seemed to be shut. Then in desperation, while very weak and almost delirious, "I made no more resolves, but cast myself upon the Lord to do with me as he should please." Forgiveness came; peace returned. "Though I have often grieved his Spirit and foolishly wandered from him since (when, alas, shall I be more wise?), his powerful grace has preserved me from such black declensions as this I have last recorded."[1]

John Newton's lesson came in a very hard way. We must not neglect the means which God gives us for knowing and maintaining a life of faith lived in the grace of God. "Are you so foolish? Having begun by the Spirit, are you now being perfected by the flesh?" (Galatians 3:3).

O Beloved, can you relate in any way to this struggle? Write out your struggle below.

DAY TWO

I pray in looking at Brownlow North and now again at how John Newton came to learn his lesson, that you and I might get a glimpse into what it means to live moment by moment or opportunity by opportunity in the grace of God rather than in the condemnation of a haunting past and in the strength of our sinful flesh.

God's same powerful grace is there to deliver you also — first, from the **penalty of sin** if you have never been saved, then second, it is there to deliver you from the **power of sin**. It is this latter aspect of living in the power of the grace of God that so many of us forget so easily.

Deliverance from the power of sin comes as you cease your striving in the flesh and cast yourself in total dependence upon Him. When you are dependent upon Him, you will find His grace is always sufficient.

We will be looking at the why and wherefore of all of this in the days to come. However, today I want to suggest that you memorize the following verses. If you will read them aloud three times daily (morning, noon, and evening) for the next week, you will find yourself able to say them from memory with ease. Reading them aloud is the key.

> And He has said to me, "My grace is sufficient for you, for power is perfected in weakness." Most gladly, therefore, I will rather boast about my weaknesses, that the power of Christ may dwell in me. Therefore I am well content with weaknesses, with insults, with distresses, with persecutions, with difficulties, for Christ's sake; for when I am weak, then I am strong (II Corinthians 12:9-10).

Having read these verses, I want to make sure that you understand them, for understanding them is a key to retaining them and being able to call them to remembrance when you need them.

1. From the text of these verses, do you see any connection between grace and power? What and why?

2. When you look at your weaknesses, how do you feel and why?

3. If you were to apply the truth of these verses to your life so that you lived in accordance with their teaching, what would you do the next time you were made aware of your weaknesses, the next time you faced your struggle, or the next time you suffered insults, distresses, persecutions, difficulties?

4. Why can you say, as Paul did, that when you are weak, it is then that you are strong?

It is my prayer that in the days and weeks ahead you will be overwhelmed by your understanding of the grace of God which has appeared to all men.

Grace and peace to you, Beloved.

DAY THREE

Failure can be overwhelming, especially if deep within your heart there is a desire to please God. You wonder how things can ever be the same between you and Him. How can you pick up the pieces and begin again?

Thoughts such as "Can God ever use me again?" "Does He even want me?" "Will things ever be the same with us?" come as "Job's friends" to chastise you, not to console you.

Have you destroyed your opportunity for a meaningful and joyous life? Are you to live forever in the shambles of your failure — existing, enduring, barely surviving rather than ever again experiencing joy, satisfaction, peace, fulfillment? Will joy ever come again?

Do thoughts such as these visit you in your stillness and engage you in conversations of "what might have been if only"?

Are you frightened by the knowledge that God is in control — wondering how He will deal with you? Do you want to run but don't know where to run? Or do you know if you choose to run that the person, the thing, the object, the situation to which you would run would only displease Him more? Does despair offer to cover you in its worn blanket of hopelessness? Do you want to hide from life's consequences, cowering in the corner of inertia?

Don't you know that you belong to the God of all grace?

Grace is God's heart laid bare. Grace is there to preserve you in the darkest night of your failures. Do not let His grace bestowed upon you through Jesus Christ be in vain. His grace — sufficient for all sin, for all failure, for all of your inadequacy, for all of your impotence — is yours to claim.

Grace is the birthright of every child of God. Grace cannot leave you inert. It calls you to get up, to throw off your blanket of hopelessness, and to move on through life in faith. **And what grace calls you to, grace provides.**

"So then, my beloved, . . . work out your salvation with fear and trembling; for it is God who is at work in you, both to will and to work for *His* good pleasure. . . . holding fast the word of life" (Philippians 2:12-13, 16a).

DAY FOUR

The kingdom of heaven is reserved for those who become as little children, for those who look to their Father in loving confidence for every benefit, whether it be for the pardon so freely given, or for the strength that comes from Him who works in them both to will and to do.[2]

How often we fail to understand this! We receive the grace of God for our salvation, but we fail to appropriate His grace which is there to cover our failure and to save us from despair which can follow on its heels. Instead, we seek to live the Christian life in our own strength and to approach God on our own merit rather than on His grace.

Grace is unmerited favor bestowed on us at the moment of our salvation. "For by grace you have been saved through faith; and that not of yourselves, *it is* the gift of God" (Ephesians 2:8).

If it took grace to save us, how can we think that it takes our own human effort and prowess to maintain us? Or how can we think that restoration is only possible through our efforts or through our merit when our own efforts weren't adequate to take care of our sin and failure in the first place?

Certainly in the family of man there is a time to leave our earthly father and mother, to strike out on our own, to make our own living, to make our own decisions as we carry out our own goals. But is this true in the family of God? Are we now so grown up that we can handle our own lives and make our own decisions, not needing God's grace any longer? Rubbish! Where does that thinking come from? Certainly not from God.

We will never cease to need our Father — His wisdom, direction, help, and support. We will never outgrow Him. We will always need His grace.

It is my prayer as we progress through this study that you will see the necessity to depend upon His grace, that you will learn to live day by day in the grace of God.

DAY FIVE

Christianity is the one and only religion in the world wherein man becomes totally dependent upon God through Jesus Christ and remains dependent upon God for every aspect of life. From its inception, the Christian life is to be lived under grace's sufficiency throughout all eternity.

To the Christian, independence is sin. Independence is the taproot of every failure in the life of the Christian.

> "Grace" in this sense is an attitude on God's part that proceeds entirely from within Himself, and that is conditioned in no way by anything in the objects of His favor.[3]

Grace goes beyond the ordinary course of what is expected, and that is why it is hard for us to accept it in our day-by-day living. We simply do not expect God to deal with us on the basis of grace. Rather, we expect Him to react as we would react, to respond as we would respond. We forget that He is God and that we are mere man. We forget to think as He would think, to learn and live by His words and not by man's reasonings and philosophies of life.

I believe grace is one of the hardest truths for us to comprehend and to live by. It is my prayer — not only for you, my friend, but for me also — that our Father would meet with us in a supernatural way. I long for the grace of God to be so engraved on our minds and hearts that we would be freed from a lifetime of attitudes, misconceptions, and independence which would keep us from appropriating His grace in all of its sufficiency.

Read Romans 12:1-2 and answer the questions that follow.

> I urge you therefore, brethren, by the mercies of God, to present your bodies a living and holy sacrifice, acceptable to God, *which is* your spiritual service of worship. And do not be conformed to this world, but be transformed by the renewing of your mind, that you may prove what the will of God is, that which is good and acceptable and perfect.

1. What is God asking you to do in these verses? Before you answer this question, let me simply say that the "therefore" is in the light of everything God has done for us through His gospel of grace.

2. According to these verses (apart from what I have already said with respect to the reason for the "therefore"), why should we do this?

3. Why should your mind be renewed? How would you apply this to what you have personally learned about the grace of God?

DAY SIX

As your mind is renewed so that you think the way God thinks rather than according to the reasoning of man, you will see your total impotence. You will see that the source of your problems is **not** poor "self-image" or lack of "self-esteem" or low "self-worth." Rather, seeing self as it is — **totally impotent and worthless apart from God** — will cause you to realize the need to continually cast yourself on the grace of God. Seeing your total poverty of spirit will cause you to be renewed in your thinking and, thus, be released from thinking that your works could ever merit favor with God. You will finally see that all you receive from God is given — freely given — without any cause within yourself.

Kenneth Wuest, in his work "Treasures from the Greek New Testament," writes:

> In the ethical terminology of the Greek schools *charis* implied ever a favor freely done, without claim or expectation of return. . . . Thus Aristotle, defining *charis*, 'lays the whole stress on this very point, that it is conferred freely, with no exception of return, and finding its only motive in the bounty and free-heartedness of the giver.'[4]

When you think of God's grace, it will help you tremendously, my friend, if you will always remember:

Grace is given; grace is free.

God's grace is freely given without any cause within myself.

Grace is always given because that is the heart of God.

Grace is always given — never owed, never earned, never a reward.

Grace is a benefit bestowed, released by faith alone.

To bring home this point, I want you to look up the following verses. Look for the word "grace"; then, record what you learn about grace.

1. Romans 12:3

2. Romans 12:6a (It is only the first part of this verse that is pertinent to your study. When I ask you to see only the first portion of a verse, I denote that by assigning to it an "a" to indicate that it is the first portion you read.)

3. Romans 15:15

Thank God for His grace and ask Him to bring these truths to your renewed mind continually, especially when you start to think or act in a way contrary to them.

Day Seven

As we learn about the grace of God, it is critically imperative that you understand that grace is not license. I cannot emphasize this enough, for there are some who would distort the doctrine of grace to their own destruction.

Grace is freely given, always bestowed, available for those who are apart from Christ and for those who already belong to Him. It is appropriated one way and only one way — by faith, nothing more, nothing less.

Yet, grace does not permit a person to live a licentious life-style. We have already seen that as a new Christian

John Newton sinned grievously. Yet, there was grace to cover his sin — grace which could not be earned, grace which could only be received by faith. If he had failed to appropriate God's grace to cover his sin and failure, I doubt that he would ever have written the hymn that has endured through the years, "Amazing Grace." Never would he have been acclaimed as a hero of the faith. Oh, yes, he would have remained a child of God, but a defeated one. Defeated Christians have little power and little effectiveness because they fail to appropriate the grace of God, for grace is power.

Although John Newton sinned, it was not his pattern of life. Remember that the covenant of grace gives the believer the indwelling Holy Spirit Who causes us to walk in His statutes and keep His commandments. What the law could not do, Jesus did by dying for us and giving us the gift of the Holy Spirit (Romans 8:1-4).

Jude was very concerned about those who distort grace. "Beloved, while I was making every effort to write you about our common salvation, I felt the necessity to write to you appealing that you contend earnestly for the faith which was once for all delivered to the saints. For certain persons have crept in unnoticed, those who were long beforehand marked out for this condemnation, ungodly persons who turn the grace of our God into licentiousness and deny our only Master and Lord, Jesus Christ" (Jude 3-4).

Licentiousness is moral anarchy. It is to live as you please. If you will notice, they deny Jesus as Master and Lord. "Lord" is *kurios*, the Greek translation of "Jehovah" in the Old Testament. "Master" is *despotēs*, one who has absolute ownership and uncontrolled power.

Do not fail to note the fate of those who turn God's grace into licentiousness! It is condemnation. These may have professed to know Jesus Christ, but by their life-style it is obvious that they never did. Let us never forget Jude 3-4 as we study the grace of God.

    1. Write out Jude 4.

    2. According to Jude 4, what is licentiousness (lasciviousness, KJV)?

    3. How do grace and licentiousness relate to one another?

    Press on, Beloved, to understand, to know, to abide in the grace of God!

Chapter 5, Notes

[1]William J. Petersen, *Johann Sebastian Bach Had a Wife* (Wheaton, Illinois: Tyndale House Publishers, Inc., 1987), p. 35-36.

[2]James Orr, ed., *The International Standard Bible Encyclopaedia*. Vol 2, 1976 reprint. (Grand Rapids, Michigan: Wm. B. Eerdmans Publishing Co., 1939), p. 1292.

[3]Orr, p. 1291.

[4]Kenneth Wuest, "Treasures from the Greek New Testament," in *Word Studies in the Greek New Testament* (Grand Rapids, Michigan: Wm. B. Eerdmans Publishing Co., 1973), III, p. 16, citing Trench, *Synonyms of the New Testament*.

*Let us therefore draw near with con-
fidence to the throne of grace, that we
may receive mercy and may find grace
to help in time of need.*
Hebrews 4:16

Grace?
To Cover Even
My Failures?

DAY ONE

Have you ever been convicted of sin and felt like an absolute dog? I have. Sometimes I groan because I know so much of the Word, yet I do not always live in the light of everything that I know. As I was writing this book, the Lord reminded me of a sin I had committed with my tongue, of an attitude which was wrong. I had to stop my writing and confess my sin.

Then, as I was going over the manuscript for *Lord, Heal My Hurts*, I was convicted again. As I read the last chapter, I came to the part on meekness. Meekness is accepting everything as coming from God without murmuring or disputing or without retaliation. I had known that definition for years. I had taught it countless times. Yet as I read what I had written, I was convicted. I had not been giving thanks in everything. When I made a mistake, I would moan and groan over my ineptness, my wrong decision, or whatever! When something would go wrong, instead of bowing my knees in submission and getting up to go on in His grace, I would hassle over the whys and wherefores.

I had become sloppy in my spiritual "attire." To fail to put on the attire of the new person I am in Christ Jesus and to fail to walk in meekness is wrong. However, to compound it with another sin is worse, and this behavior leads to a downward spiral that will crash in defeat and despair if we don't pull out of our nosedive by leveling out in grace. I hate it when I sin, and that is the way it should be. But many times, because my flesh wants to "be perfect," I have the awful tendency to stew over my lack of perfection and "what could have been if only" I had obeyed God in the first place. That should not be.

When this kind of mental stewing begins, one can fail in the grace of God also. You become like a plane diving headlong toward the ground, spinning round and round in your "if only's." You need to grab the stick and pull it back. That stick is grace! I am sure that at one time or another you have seen a war movie where the pilot is in a daze, headed for the ground while the audience is on the edge of their seats saying, "Pull back! Pull it back!" Grace is the stick, the lever of life that keeps you on a steady course.

When I confess my sin, I need to go forward believing what God says — that He is faithful and just to forgive all my sins and to cleanse me from all unrighteousness (I John 1:9). However, if I then begin to mentally hash over the consequences of my sin or to focus on "if only" or "why didn't I," I am failing of the grace of God, grace which is sufficient to override what I fail to discern, to distinguish, or what I do not get done.

Now let me bring all of this to an applicable conclusion so that you don't miss what you need to see.

What can you do when you see all of this?
> You can defend yourself.
>
> You can excuse yourself.
>
> You can rationalize your sin by saying that you have been under too much pressure or too much "whatever."
>
> You can cover it. Just ignore it. Not face it. Deny it.
>
> You can blame others. (Isn't this easy to do — to say that it is "so and so's" fault? Because if he hadn't, you wouldn't have!)
>
> You can struggle, try harder to be a better Christian.

Any of these responses is to fail of the grace of God. The message of the gospel of grace is that you can never, ever create a righteousness of your own that could ever please God.

THINK ABOUT IT.

Day Two

One of the greatest needs among true Christians today is to learn how to deal with their sin once they have failed God in this way. So often they feel that God will turn away from them in anger, that the forgiveness that is theirs through grace will eventually be dried up. Or they feel that one day God will have had enough and will walk away, for His patience will have come to an end. This kind of thinking is understandable if we measure God by man. The cure is a renewed mind whereby we measure God by what God says about Himself in His Word rather than by man's concept of Him.

When a child of God sins, he can run either to Mount Calvary or to Mount Sinai. Calvary was the mountain where God inaugurated the covenant of grace as He put to death His Son, the covenant Lamb. Sinai was the mountain on which the law was inaugurated as Moses "took the blood of the calves and the goats, with water and scarlet wool and hyssop, and sprinkled both the book itself and all the people, saying, 'THIS IS THE BLOOD OF THE COVENANT WHICH GOD COMMANDED YOU'" (Hebrews 9:19-20).

To run to Mount Sinai is to try to rectify your failure or your sin by yourself by defending, excusing, rationalizing, covering, or blaming your sin on someone else. If all of that didn't work before, what makes you think it will work now? Sin and failure cannot be covered. It must be atoned for.

Or when you see your own impotence, weakness, and insufficiency and you struggle and try harder and harder to be better, to be the Christian you should be, then you are running to Mount Sinai.

Let's think this through. If you couldn't be saved apart from grace, why do you think that you can live a life pleasing to God in your own strength, in your own ability?

Running to Mount Sinai is not going to help at all. As a matter of fact, it will compound your problem, for it will bring misery and not peace. It will bring frustration rather than victory. **Victory never comes through the law.**

You **must** run to Mount Calvary! GRACE, BELOVED; **GRACE IS WHAT YOU NEED!**

How does one run to Mount Calvary and there bathe in the cleansing power of the blood of the new covenant?

First, appropriate His grace by agreeing with God. Call sin exactly what it is. Agree with God that it is wrong. Confess to God aloud with your lips. "If we say that we have no sin, we are deceiving ourselves, and the truth is not in us. If we confess our sins, He is faithful and righteous to forgive us our sins and to cleanse us from all unrighteousness" (I John 1:8-9).

Then, don't struggle to be better. Don't determine that you are going to try harder. Merely acknowledge your need of His all-sufficient grace and go forward trusting in the grace of God. "As you therefore have received Christ Jesus the Lord, *so* walk in Him" (Colossians 2:6). You were saved by faith; therefore, you are to walk in faith. It may be one step at a time, but walk. You can say, "I can't," as long as in the next breath you say, "But, God, You can."

DAY THREE

Do you ever feel that you just can't be holy? Do you think that holiness is for the super saints, not ordinary Christians?

Maybe you have even compiled a whole list of dos and don'ts, things you think spiritual people would or wouldn't do. You won't miss church, visitation, Sunday School meetings. You are working hard doing everything you're asked to do for Jesus and the church. You have tried to be super spiritual, but you feel like quitting, for it's not doing one bit of good. You might be able to list a lot of accomplishments on your biographical sketch as a Christian, but you know it would be mostly all words.

You know what goes on inside. You know what you struggle with. You know that you fail when the doors are shut, when others are not around.

The book of Galatians just might have the answer for you. We looked at the third chapter when we studied the purpose of the old covenant. Now I want us to look at the fourth chapter.

Galatians was written because some people went into the region of Galatia preaching a different gospel than the one that they had heard from Paul. The message they proclaimed taught that you might be saved by faith in Jesus Christ but that you still had to be circumcised and live under the law. In essence, they were calling Christians to become proselytes of Judaism, saying that grace through faith was not sufficient if they wanted to maintain their justification. These false teachers were declaring that justification is obtained through the Cross of Christ but that it is maintained through the law. Because they did not denounce Christ or His work on Calvary, their teaching was not easy to detect as "another gospel" (Galatians 1:6-9).

While you may not be hearing exactly the same message, still many of its seeds have drifted down through the centuries. And various mutations have blown into the garden of our thinking and taken root there. Consequently, we feel that somehow or another we can gain acceptance or favor with God by keeping a certain code of dos or don'ts or by our good works. Such thoughts need to be uprooted, for they choke out grace.

Read through the book of Galatians printed out for you. It is only six chapters long, and you will find it profitable for your soul, my friend. I would suggest that you mark the following words in a distinctive way or color so that you can spot their occurrence at a glance:

a. grace
b. gospel
c. faith
d. law
e. promise
f. Spirit

Tomorrow we will look at Mount Calvary and Mount Sinai. See if you can find the specific passage in Galatians that we are going to study.

GALATIANS

Chapter 1

1 Paul, an apostle (not *sent* from men, nor through the agency of man, but through Jesus Christ, and God the Father, who raised Him from the dead),

2 and all the brethren who are with me, to the churches of Galatia:

3 Grace to you and peace from God our Father, and the Lord Jesus Christ,

4 who gave Himself for our sins, that He might deliver us out of this present evil age, according to the will of our God and Father,

5 to whom *be* the glory forevermore. Amen.

6 I am amazed that you are so quickly deserting Him who called you by the grace of Christ, for a different gospel;

7 which is *really* not another; only there are some who are disturbing you, and want to distort the gospel of Christ.

8 But even though we, or an angel from heaven, should preach to you a gospel contrary to that which we have preached to you, let him be accursed.

9 As we have said before, so I say again now, if any man is preaching to you a gospel contrary to that which you received, let him be accursed.

10 For am I now seeking the favor of men, or of God? Or am I striving to please men? If I were still trying to please men, I would not be a bond-servant of Christ.

11 For I would have you know, brethren, that the gospel which was preached by me is not according to man.

12 For I neither received it from man, nor was I taught it, but *I received it* through a revelation of Jesus Christ.

13 For you have heard of my former manner of life in Judaism, how I used to persecute the church of God beyond measure, and tried to destroy it;

14 and I was advancing in Judaism beyond many of my contemporaries among my countrymen, being more extremely zealous for my ancestral traditions.

15 But when He who had set me apart, *even* from my mother's womb, and called me through His grace, was pleased

16 to reveal His Son in me, that I might preach Him among the Gentiles, I did not immediately consult with flesh and blood,

17 nor did I go up to Jerusalem to those who were apostles before me; but I went away to Arabia, and returned once more to Damascus.

18 Then three years later I went up to Jerusalem to become acquainted with Cephas, and stayed with him fifteen days.

19 But I did not see any other of the apostles except James, the Lord's brother.

20 (Now in what I am writing to you, I assure you before God *that* I am not lying.)

21 Then I went into the regions of Syria and Cilicia.

22 And I was *still* unknown by sight to the churches of Judea which were in Christ;

23 but only, they kept hearing, "He who once persecuted us is now preaching the faith which he once tried to destroy."

24 And they were glorifying God because of me.

Chapter 2

1 Then after an interval of fourteen years I went up again to Jerusalem with Barnabas, taking Titus along also.

2 And it was because of a revelation that I went up; and I submitted to them the gospel which I preach among the Gentiles, but I did so in private to those who were

of reputation, for fear that I might be running, or had run, in vain.

3 But not even Titus who was with me, though he was a Greek, was compelled to be circumcised.

4 But *it was* because of the false brethren who had sneaked in to spy out our liberty which we have in Christ Jesus, in order to bring us into bondage.

5 But we did not yield in subjection to them for even an hour, so that the truth of the gospel might remain with you.

6 But from those who were of high reputation (what they were makes no difference to me; God shows no partiality) — well, those who were of reputation contributed nothing to me.

7 But on the contrary, seeing that I had been entrusted with the gospel to the uncircumcised, just as Peter *had been* to the circumcised

8 (for He who effectually worked for Peter in *his* apostleship to the circumcised effectually worked for me also to the Gentiles),

9 and recognizing the grace that had been given to me, James and Cephas and John, who were reputed to be pillars, gave to me and Barnabas the right hand of fellowship, that we might go to the Gentiles, and they to the circumcised.

10 *They* only *asked* us to remember the poor — the very thing I also was eager to do.

11 But when Cephas came to Antioch, I opposed him to his face, because he stood condemned.

12 For prior to the coming of certain men from James, he used to eat with the Gentiles; but when they came, he *began* to withdraw and hold himself aloof, fearing the party of the circumcision.

13 And the rest of the Jews joined him in hypocrisy, with the result that even Barnabas was carried away by their hypocrisy.

14 But when I saw that they were not straightforward about the truth of the gospel, I said to Cephas in the presence of all, "If you, being a Jew, live like the Gentiles and not like the Jews, how *is it that* you compel the Gentiles to live like Jews?

15 "We *are* Jews by nature, and not sinners from among the Gentiles;

16 nevertheless knowing that a man is not justified by the works of the Law but through faith in Christ Jesus, even we have believed in Christ Jesus, that we may be justified by faith in Christ, and not by the works of the Law; since by the works of the Law shall no flesh be justified.

17 "But if, while seeking to be justified in Christ, we ourselves have also been found sinners, is Christ then a minister of sin? May it never be!

18 "For if I rebuild what I have *once* destroyed, I prove myself to be a transgressor.

19 "For through the Law I died to the Law, that I might live to God.

20 "I have been crucified with Christ; and it is no longer I who live, but Christ lives in me; and the *life* which I now live in the flesh I live by faith in the Son of God, who loved me, and delivered Himself up for me.

21 "I do not nullify the grace of God; for if righteousness *comes* through the Law, then Christ died needlessly."

Chapter 3

1 You foolish Galatians, who has bewitched you, before whose eyes Jesus Christ was publicly portrayed *as* crucified?

2 This is the only thing I want to find out from you: did you receive the Spirit by the works of the Law, or by hearing with faith?

3 Are you so foolish? Having begun by the Spirit, are you now being perfected by the flesh?

4 Did you suffer so many things in vain — if indeed it was in vain?

5 Does He then, who provides you with the Spirit and works miracles among you, do it by the works of the Law, or by hearing with faith?

6 Even so Abraham BELIEVED GOD, AND IT WAS RECKONED TO HIM AS RIGHTEOUSNESS.

7 Therefore, be sure that it is those who are of faith who are sons of Abraham.

8 And the Scripture, foreseeing that God would justify the Gentiles by faith, preached the gospel beforehand to Abraham, *saying*, "ALL THE NATIONS SHALL BE BLESSED IN YOU."

9 So then those who are of faith are blessed with Abraham, the believer.

10 For as many as are of the works of the Law are under a curse; for it is written, "CURSED IS EVERYONE WHO DOES NOT ABIDE BY ALL THINGS WRITTEN IN THE BOOK OF THE LAW, TO PERFORM THEM."

11 Now that no one is justified by the Law before God is evident; for, "THE RIGHTEOUS MAN SHALL LIVE BY FAITH."

12 However, the Law is not of faith; on the contrary, "HE WHO PRACTICES THEM SHALL LIVE BY THEM."

13 Christ redeemed us from the curse of the Law, having become a curse for us — for it is written, "CURSED IS EVERYONE WHO HANGS ON A TREE" —

14 in order that in Christ Jesus the blessing of Abraham might come to the Gentiles, so that we might receive the promise of the Spirit through faith.

15 Brethren, I speak in terms of human relations: even though it is *only* a man's covenant, yet when it has been ratified, no one sets it aside or adds conditions to it.

16 Now the promises were spoken to Abraham and to his seed. He does not say, "And to seeds," as *referring* to many, but *rather* to one, "And to your seed," that is, Christ.

17 What I am saying is this: the Law, which came four hundred and thirty years later, does not invalidate a

covenant previously ratified by God, so as to nullify the promise.

18 For if the inheritance is based on law, it is no longer based on a promise; but God has granted it to Abraham by means of a promise.

19 Why the Law then? It was added because of transgressions, having been ordained through angels by the agency of a mediator, until the seed should come to whom the promise had been made.

20 Now a mediator is not for one *party only*; whereas God is *only* one.

21 Is the Law then contrary to the promises of God? May it never be! For if a law had been given which was able to impart life, then righteousness would indeed have been based on law.

22 But the Scripture has shut up all men under sin, that the promise by faith in Jesus Christ might be given to those who believe.

23 But before faith came, we were kept in custody under the law, being shut up to the faith which was later to be revealed.

24 Therefore the Law has become our tutor *to lead us* to Christ, that we may be justified by faith.

25 But now that faith has come, we are no longer under a tutor.

26 For you are all sons of God through faith in Christ Jesus.

27 For all of you who were baptized into Christ have clothed yourselves with Christ.

28 There is neither Jew nor Greek, there is neither slave nor free man, there is neither male nor female; for you are all one in Christ Jesus.

29 And if you belong to Christ, then you are Abraham's offspring, heirs according to promise.

Chapter 4

1 Now I say, as long as the heir is a child, he does not differ at all from a slave although he is owner of everything,

2 but he is under guardians and managers until the date set by the father.

3 So also we, while we were children, were held in bondage under the elemental things of the world.

4 But when the fulness of the time came, God sent forth His Son, born of a woman, born under the Law,

5 in order that He might redeem those who were under the Law, that we might receive the adoption as sons.

6 And because you are sons, God has sent forth the Spirit of His Son into our hearts, crying, "Abba! Father!"

7 Therefore you are no longer a slave, but a son; and if a son, then an heir through God.

8 However at that time, when you did not know God, you were slaves to those which by nature are no gods.

9 But now that you have come to know God, or rather to be known by God, how is it that you turn back again to the weak and worthless elemental things, to which you desire to be enslaved all over again?

10 You observe days and months and seasons and years.

11 I fear for you, that perhaps I have labored over you in vain.

12 I beg of you, brethren, become as I *am*, for I also *have become* as you *are*. You have done me no wrong;

13 but you know that it was because of a bodily illness that I preached the gospel to you the first time;

14 and that which was a trial to you in my bodily condition you did not despise or loathe, but you received me as an angel of God, as Christ Jesus *Himself*.

15 Where then is that sense of blessing you had? For I bear you witness, that if possible, you would have plucked out your eyes and given them to me.

16 Have I therefore become your enemy by telling you the truth?

17 They eagerly seek you, not commendably, but they wish to shut you out, in order that you may seek them.

18 But it is good always to be eagerly sought in a commendable manner, and not only when I am present with you.

19 My children, with whom I am again in labor until Christ is formed in you —

20 but I could wish to be present with you now and to change my tone, for I am perplexed about you.

21 Tell me, you who want to be under law, do you not listen to the law?

22 For it is written that Abraham had two sons, one by the bondwoman and one by the free woman.

23 But the son by the bondwoman was born according to the flesh, and the son by the free woman through the promise.

24 This is allegorically speaking: for these *women* are two covenants, one *proceeding* from Mount Sinai bearing children who are to be slaves; she is Hagar.

25 Now this Hagar is Mount Sinai in Arabia, and corresponds to the present Jerusalem, for she is in slavery with her children.

26 But the Jerusalem above is free; she is our mother.

27 For it is written,

"REJOICE, BARREN WOMAN WHO DOES NOT BEAR;

BREAK FORTH AND SHOUT, YOU WHO ARE NOT IN LABOR;

FOR MORE ARE THE CHILDREN OF THE DESOLATE

THAN OF THE ONE WHO HAS A HUSBAND."

28 And you brethren, like Isaac, are children of promise.

29 But as at that time he who was born according to the flesh persecuted him *who was born* according to the Spirit, so it is now also.

30 But what does the Scripture say?

"CAST OUT THE BONDWOMAN AND HER SON,

FOR THE SON OF THE BONDWOMAN SHALL NOT BE AN HEIR

WITH THE SON OF THE FREE WOMAN."

31 So then, brethren, we are not children of a bondwoman, but of the free woman.

Chapter 5

1 It was for freedom that Christ set us free; therefore keep standing firm and do not be subject again to a yoke of slavery.

2 Behold I, Paul, say to you that if you receive circumcision, Christ will be of no benefit to you.

3 And I testify again to every man who receives circumcision, that he is under obligation to keep the whole Law.

4 You have been severed from Christ, you who are seeking to be justified by law; you have fallen from grace.

5 For we through the Spirit, by faith, are waiting for the hope of righteousness.

6 For in Christ Jesus neither circumcision nor uncircumcision means anything, but faith working through love.

7 You were running well; who hindered you from obeying the truth?

8 This persuasion *did* not *come* from Him who calls you.

9 A little leaven leavens the whole lump *of dough.*

10 I have confidence in you in the Lord, that you will adopt no other view; but the one who is disturbing you shall bear his judgment, whoever he is.

11 But I, brethren, if I still preach circumcision, why am I still persecuted? Then the stumbling block of the cross has been abolished.

12 Would that those who are troubling you would even mutilate themselves.

13 For you were called to freedom, brethren; only *do* not *turn* your freedom into an opportunity for the flesh, but through love serve one another.

14 For the whole Law is fulfilled in one word, in the *statement,* "YOU SHALL LOVE YOUR NEIGHBOR AS YOURSELF."

15 But if you bite and devour one another, take care lest you be consumed by one another.

16 But I say, walk by the Spirit, and you will not carry out the desire of the flesh.

17 For the flesh sets its desire against the Spirit, and the Spirit against the flesh; for these are in opposition to one another, so that you may not do the things that you please.

18 But if you are led by the Spirit, you are not under the Law.

19 Now the deeds of the flesh are evident, which are: immorality, impurity, sensuality,

20 idolatry, sorcery, enmities, strife, jealousy, outbursts of anger, disputes, dissensions, factions,

21 envying, drunkenness, carousing, and things like these, of which I forewarn you just as I have forewarned you that those who practice such things shall not inherit the kingdom of God.

22 But the fruit of the Spirit is love, joy, peace, patience, kindness, goodness, faithfulness,

23 gentleness, self-control; against such things there is no law.

24 Now those who belong to Christ Jesus have crucified the flesh with its passions and desires.

25 If we live by the Spirit, let us also walk by the Spirit.

26 Let us not become boastful, challenging one another, envying one another.

Chapter 6

1 Brethren, even if a man is caught in any trespass, you who are spiritual, restore such a one in a spirit of gentleness; *each one* looking to yourself, lest you too be tempted.

2 Bear one another's burdens, and thus fulfill the law of Christ.

3 For if anyone thinks he is something when he is nothing, he deceives himself.

4 But let each one examine his own work, and then he will have *reason for* boasting in regard to himself alone, and not in regard to another.

5 For each one shall bear his own load.

6 And let the one who is taught the word share all good things with him who teaches.

7 Do not be deceived, God is not mocked; for whatever a man sows, this he will also reap.

8 For the one who sows to his own flesh shall from the flesh reap corruption, but the one who sows to the Spirit shall from the Spirit reap eternal life.

9 And let us not lose heart in doing good, for in due time we shall reap if we do not grow weary.

10 So then, while we have opportunity, let us do good to all men, and especially to those who are of the household of the faith.

11 See with what large letters I am writing to you with my own hand.

12 Those who desire to make a good showing in the flesh try to compel you to be circumcised, simply that they may not be persecuted for the cross of Christ.

13 For those who are circumcised do not even keep the Law themselves, but they desire to have you circumcised, that they may boast in your flesh.

14 But may it never be that I should boast, except in the cross of our Lord Jesus Christ, through which the world has been crucified to me, and I to the world.

15 For neither is circumcision anything, nor uncircumcision, but a new creation.

16 And those who will walk by this rule, peace and mercy *be* upon them, and upon the Israel of God.

17 From now on let no one cause trouble for me, for I bear on my body the brand-marks of Jesus.

18 The grace of our Lord Jesus Christ be with your spirit, brethren. Amen.

DAY FOUR

How did you do in Galatians yesterday? It's an interesting and much-needed book — especially in a society that is so caught up in the world and in humanism whereby man thinks he can do anything.

Did you find the contrast between the two mountains? We will look at it in-depth today.

Carefully read Galatians 4:21-5:1. Go back to yesterday where Galatians is printed out for you so that you can mark some key words in this particular segment. Read this passage aloud several times. It will help you remember and understand it better.

In a distinctive way or color, mark each occurrence of the following words and phrases:
   a. law
   b. according to the flesh
   c. according to the Spirit
   d. free
   e. slaves, slavery
   f. bondwoman
   g. covenants

Think on these verses, and we will discuss them tomorrow. Today thank our God for the freedom He provided in Christ Jesus.

DAY FIVE

Do you remember how it came about that Abraham had two sons? Just so we won't miss the liberating truth Paul wants us to see in Galatians 4:21-5:1, let's do a quick review of Abraham's life. How well it demonstrates again the grace of God!

Abraham was originally called Abram. He lived in Ur of the Chaldeans and was a worshiper of idols. When, by His grace, God called Abram, He promised a childless man and his wife, Sarai, that He would make of him a great nation (Genesis 12). At the time, Abram was 75 years old and Sarai was 65. The promise of a "seed" to Abram and Sarai was not given just once. It was confirmed to Abram in a covenant agreement where God, in the form of a smoking oven and a flaming torch, passed through the pieces of the covenant sacrifice (Genesis 15).

When Abram was 85 or 86, Sarai grew tired of waiting on God's promise. She was still barren. Convinced that God was going to execute His promise another way, she reasoned in her mind that if Abram were to go in to her maid Hagar and have a child by her, it would be considered Sarai's child as well as Abram's. "So Sarai said to Abram, 'Now behold, the LORD has prevented me from bearing *children*. Please go in to my maid; perhaps I shall obtain children through her.' And Abram listened to the voice of Sarai. And he went in to Hagar, and she conceived; and when she saw that she had conceived, her mistress was despised in her sight. And Abram was eighty-six years old when Hagar bore Ishmael to him" (Genesis 16:2, 4, 16).

"Now when Abram was ninety-nine years old, the LORD appeared to Abram and said to him, 'I am God Almighty; walk before Me, and be blameless. And I will establish My covenant between Me and you, and I will multiply you exceedingly.' And Abram fell on his face, and God talked with him, saying, 'As for Me, behold, My covenant is with you, and you shall be the father of a multitude of nations. No longer shall your name be called Abram, but your name shall be Abraham; for I will make you the father of a multitude of nations.' Then God said to Abraham, 'As for Sarai your wife, you shall not call her name Sarai, but Sarah *shall be* her name. And I will bless her, and indeed I will give you a son by her. Then I will bless her, and she shall be *a mother of* nations; kings of peoples shall come from her.' Then Abraham fell on his face and laughed, and said in his heart, 'Will a child be born to a man one hundred years old? And will Sarah, who is ninety years old, bear *a child*?' And Abraham said to God, 'Oh that Ishmael might live before Thee!' But God said, 'No, but Sarah your wife shall bear you a son, and you shall call his name Isaac; and I will establish My covenant with him for an everlasting covenant for his descendants after him'" (Genesis 17:1-5, 15-19).

"Now Abraham was one hundred years old when his son Isaac was born to him. And the child grew and was weaned, and Abraham made a great feast on the day that Isaac was weaned. Now Sarah saw the son of Hagar the Egyptian, whom she had borne to Abraham, mocking. Therefore she said to Abraham, 'Drive out this maid and her son, for the son of this maid shall not be an heir with my son Isaac.' And the matter distressed Abraham greatly because of his son. But God said to Abraham, 'Do not be distressed because of the lad and your maid; whatever Sarah tells you, listen to her, for through Isaac your descendants shall be named'" (Genesis 21:5, 8-12).

As you read these accounts in Genesis, aren't you awed with God and His Word? First God moves in His sovereignty in people's lives, and then later He uses the accounts of His workings allegorically to give us a precept by which we are to continuously live!

What is your assignment for today? I want you to parallel what you observed yesterday with what you read today. Write down what you see without adding anything to the text. Don't let your imagination run wild, but simply see what the Scriptures are saying.

DAY SIX

When Paul wrote to those at Rome, he explained in great detail the gospel of grace. Wanting to make sure that they understood that justification would be by grace alone and not by works or by circumcision or by the law, he chose Abraham as his chief witness. In Romans Chapter 4, Paul uses Abraham's faith in waiting for Isaac as an example.

Let me jump right into this chapter and quote what Paul says, then I will explain the passage and show you how it fits with Galatians Chapter 4. Watch for the words "grace," "faith," and "promise." In fact, you may want to mark them.

Romans 4:16-21

16 For this reason *it is* by faith, that *it might be* in accordance with grace, in order that the promise may be certain to all the descendants [Lit., *seed*], not only to those who are of the Law, but also to those who are of the faith of Abraham, who is the father of us all,

17 (as it is written, "A FATHER OF MANY NATIONS HAVE I MADE YOU") in the sight of Him whom he believed, *even* God, who gives life to the dead and calls into being that which does not exist.

18 In hope against hope he believed, in order that he might become a father of many nations, according to that which had been spoken, "SO SHALL YOUR DESCENDANTS BE."

19 And without becoming weak in faith he contemplated his own body, now as good as dead since he was about a hundred years old, and the deadness of Sarah's womb;

20 yet, with respect to the promise of God, he did not

waver in unbelief, but grew strong in faith, giving

glory to God,

21 and being fully assured that what He had promised, He

was able also to perform.

What do you need to remember about grace with respect to dealing with sin when it occurs in your life? You need to remember that you are under grace, not law. You need to remember that you are under grace alone, not grace **and** law. Like Abraham, you are not to look at what you see or what you feel. You are to look at the promises of God which are "yea and amen." What God promises, He is able to perform. In your case, God promises cleansing and forgiveness. "There is therefore now no condemnation for those who are in Christ Jesus" (Romans 8:1).

Therefore, if you feel condemned, if you feel you must do something to make amends, to pay for your sin, to do penance, you must remember that those are feelings. Feelings have nothing to do with faith. Faith is taking God at His Word, no matter how you feel or what you see or think. When God speaks clearly in His Word, you must not allow anything else to crowd out faith.

Cast out the bondwoman and her son! They represent the law. And living under law **and** grace together is impossible. If it's law, it cannot be grace. If it's grace, it cannot be law. "It was for freedom that Christ set us free; therefore keep standing firm and do not be subject again to a yoke of slavery" (Galatians 5:1). You are a child of the free woman. **GRACE IS HER NAME!** She became your mother through the promise, not through works or law or because God owed you a thing.

To be a child of the bondwoman is to be in slavery. That, Beloved, is what people are in when they try to come to God on any other basis than grace. People who cannot accept the fact that God will hear their confession and cleanse them from all unrighteousness chain themselves to impotence.

DAY SEVEN

To think you can do something to assist God in dealing with your sin is pride. Pride immediately shuts off the flow of grace.

"GOD IS OPPOSED TO THE PROUD, BUT GIVES GRACE TO THE HUMBLE" (James 4:6).

This is a Scripture which you must not forget. Pride shuts the door to the grace of God because grace, as we have seen, is given to the poor in spirit. It is given to those who see their own wretchedness, their impotence to be good or to produce anything that is good. "No one is good except God alone" (Mark 10:18b). **It is grace alone which makes us accepted in the Beloved** (Ephesians 1:6, KJV).

One of the greatest books in all the world next to the Bible was written by a man who wrestled for years with this truth. But once he saw the truth, the pilgrim made progress on his journey to the celestial city. John Bunyan's struggle to understand and accept the grace of God is common to many who, like him, see their sin but feel that they in themselves have to do something about it in order to be accepted by God.

Whether it is grace for salvation or grace to cover our sins as a Christian, it is only given to those who will humble themselves before God.

"Submit therefore to God. Resist the devil and he will flee from you. Draw near to God **and He will draw near to you.** Cleanse your hands, you sinners; and purify your hearts, you double-minded. Be miserable and mourn and weep; let your laughter be turned into mourning, and your joy to gloom. Humble yourselves in the presence of the Lord, and He will exalt you" (James 4:7-10).

Do these last verses that I quoted from James seem contrary to your understanding of the grace of God? I can understand that. However, Scripture cannot contradict itself. Therefore, let me explain what I believe God is saying to us. James's words are a necessary caution which we must keep before us whenever we study the grace of God. Here James shows us what our attitude should be towards our sin. We shouldn't sin and then laugh about it. Even though we are children of God and the penalty of sin has been paid, we must never treat sin lightly. The grace of God cost God His Son.

Grace is not license. Grace does not allow us to live in willful, continuous rebellion against God. Romans 6:14-15 states, "For sin shall not be master over you, for you are not under law, but under grace. What then? Shall we sin because we are not under law but under grace? May it never be!"

Grace delivers us from sin's reign. God wants us to remember that. Thus, He puts a frightening warning before our eyes in Hebrews 10:26-29: "For if we go on sinning willfully after receiving the knowledge of the truth, there no longer remains a sacrifice for sins, but a certain terrifying expectation of judgment, and THE FURY OF A FIRE WHICH WILL CONSUME THE ADVERSARIES. Anyone who has set aside the Law of Moses dies without mercy on *the testimony of* two or three witnesses. How much severer punishment do you think he will deserve who has trampled under foot the Son of God, and has regarded as unclean the blood of the covenant by which he was sanctified, and has insulted the Spirit of grace?"

If one says that Jesus's sacrifice is not adequate to care for our sin, or if he flagrantly continues in willful sin, thinking, "I am under grace, so what?" he is insulting the Spirit of grace. He can know that he does not understand the grace of God or the salvation that it brings. He is blind to grace and open to the judgment of God.

The truths which I am sharing with you, my friend, are not lightly understood; yet they are essential to those who would go on to maturity in Christ Jesus and the Christlikeness it brings. Therefore, think on them. Meditate on them, and as you read God's Word day in and day out, bring them before the plumb line of the **whole** counsel of His Word.

"And since *we have* a great priest over the house of God, let us draw near with a sincere heart in full assurance of faith, having our hearts sprinkled *clean* from an evil conscience and our bodies washed with pure water. Let us hold fast the confession of our hope without wavering, for He who promised is faithful" (Hebrews 10:21-23).

"Grace be with all those who love our Lord Jesus Christ with *a love* incorruptible" (Ephesians 6:24).

But by the grace of God I am what I am, and His grace toward me did not prove vain; but I labored even more than all of them, yet not I, but the grace of God with me.
I Corinthians 15:10

Grace?
To Cover All I was
and All I Am?

DAY ONE

Tonight he would murder the Queen. Slipping undetected into her bedroom, he went straight to his hiding place — the mammoth walnut wardrobe. Behind the softness of a velvet gown which covered his presence, once more he rehearsed his plan. He would know when the Queen had retired, for her maid-in-waiting would bid her good night upon leaving her room. He knew he could easily hear the door shut. It was a heavy door which shut with a bang. It irritated the Queen, but she would not give up her fresh air which created the vacuum that caused the door to always close with a thud.

Through the crack in the wardrobe door, which kept him from suffocating among the thicknesses of her gowns, he would be able to tell when the Queen blew out the candle beside her bed.

He would wait for her breathing to change. Then he would slip out quietly in his stocking feet, walk to the bed, and rid England of her Queen.

The very rehearsing of his plan put him at ease. Loosening his grip on his dagger, he dropped his arm to his side. He leaned back against the strong boards of the ornately carved wardrobe to wait. It would be a while before the Queen even retired.

Suddenly the door of the armoire opened and a huge hand, fingers spread open wide, touched him. Touching a warm, sweaty human was unexpected, but the groping hand immediately grabbed its surprise by the shirt. In all of his planning the assassin forgot one thing — the Queen's room was thoroughly searched each night before she went to bed. He was wrenched from seclusion.

As the would-be murderer was brought before Queen Elizabeth, he dropped to his knees and began to plead with her that she might extend to him her grace.

"Sir, if I extend unto you my grace, what do you promise for the future?"

With the keenest insight of theologians, the man answered, "Your Majesty, your Majesty, a grace that propositions and a grace that bargains is no grace at all!"

Astute in her understanding of grace, the Queen, seeing the truth of the man's bold response, said, "Sir, freely, by my grace, I forgive you." Grace freely given won a convert. From that point on, the man was the most devoted servant the Queen ever had.

This week we are going to look at the grace that serves, laboring in its King's service.

"But by the grace of God I am what I am, and His grace toward me did not prove vain; but I labored even more than all of them, yet not I, but the grace of God with me" (I Corinthians 15:10).

DAY TWO

Grace is active. And because it is, you and I are able to live productive lives which have eternal significance. This is an important fact to understand, for often we think of grace as merely doctrine that explains our salvation, something which occurred and is over. But grace is power in action. Oh, if we could only get this into our heads and then into our daily living, what passion it would bring to our service to Him and for Him!

Remember we saw that grace is all of God. Man just becomes the vessel to contain the grace of God. Consequently, when it comes to a life of obedience and service, even the desire and the power to obey and to serve God come from Him. Philippians 2:13 teaches us that "it is God who is at work in you, both to will and to work for *His* good pleasure." Think on it!

God is saying that our motivation to live for Him comes from Him! And our ability to do what He desires us to do comes from Him! **It is all of grace!**

Desiring and doing or working are not passive but active. Grace is active. It is power in action — God's power! I should throw in a whole line of exclamation points!

As you think about this, you may wonder, "If this is true about grace, why aren't Christians having a greater impact on their world?" That's a good question. The answer is found in Philippians 2:12, the verse which precedes this truth.

"So then, my beloved, just as you have always obeyed, not as in my presence only, but now much more in my absence, work out your salvation with fear and trembling; for it is God who is at work in you, both to will and to work for *His* good pleasure" (Philippians 2:12-13).

We are not seeing Christians have a greater impact, because they are the bottleneck! In verse 12 God doesn't tell us to work **for** our salvation; He tells us to work **out** our salvation. We are to carry out to completion that which God works in us. Philippians 2:12-13 assures us that God not only gives us the desire to do His good pleasure but that He gives us the ability to do it. You will see grace in action when God's children pull out the stops and let God be God in all of His power!

DAY THREE

Basically there are three commands given to the child of God with respect to his or her relationship with the Holy Spirit. Look them up and write them out. Note what we are commanded to do with respect to our relationship with the Holy Spirit.

1. Ephesians 5:18

2. I Thessalonians 5:19

3. Ephesians 4:30

The verb "be filled" in Ephesians 5:18 is a present passive imperative verb. In the other two verses, the verbs "quench" and "grieve" are present active imperative. The present tense denotes continuous or habitual action. The active voice indicates that the subject produces the action of the main verb. The passive voice means that the subject receives the action of the main verb. The imperative mood means that it is a command. In the light of these insights, look at these verses again. Next to each verse, record who does the action and who is responsible to see that it happens.

As you have probably seen, it is the quenching of the Holy Spirit which keeps us from walking in the power of God's grace. To **not** carry out to completion what God is working in you both to will and do of **His** good pleasure is to quench the Holy Spirit. To do that which is contrary to the Holy Spirit or to the character or commandments of God is to grieve the Holy Spirit. To be filled with the Holy Spirit is to allow Him to have full control.

O Beloved, where do you stand with the Spirit of God? Is God's grace seen in your life?

DAY FOUR

One of the ways in which God's grace is seen in our lives, apart from salvation, is in our service for Him. However, to some, service may seem to be the opposite of grace.

Sometimes spiritual sayings become popular among different groups of Christians. Often these become very good reminders of truths that we need to concentrate on. However, there are times when phrases can throw our walk off balance because we carry them to an extreme. Or we negate other truths with these sayings because we forget to consider the whole counsel of God.

One of the sayings that I have heard quite a bit is, "God is not interested in what you do; He's interested in what you are." Another one that is similar to this is, "It's not doing, but being."

It is true that God is interested in who and what we are. He cares about what I am like on the inside, and if I serve Him without becoming like Him, something is wrong. However, if we are what we ought to be, our lives will find expression in service for God. It may not be something that others would necessarily see or recognize, but it will be there.

Grace may call you to prayer. Grace may be expressed simply in your speech. Or it may be manifested through the gift of helps, mercy, or any of the other gifts listed in the Word of God. But it will be expressed in its activity. Why? Grace is active, and it will become active in and through you. Your responsibility is to carry out what God works in. He will be responsible for its impact. Wow! Isn't that exciting!

Let's look at I Corinthians 15:9-10: "For I am the least of the apostles, who am not fit to be called an apostle, because I persecuted the church of God. But by the grace of God I am what I am, and His grace toward me did not prove vain; but I labored even more than all of them, yet not I, but the grace of God with me."

As you read these verses, did you notice what I call colaboring in the work of God? Paul says that he labors more than others, yet it is not his laboring, but the grace of God with him. See how beautifully this fits with Philippians 2:12-13?

Paul understood grace! Here was a man who missed the earthly ministry of Christ, who was a persecutor and murderer of Christians, and who considered himself the chief of sinners and the least of the Apostles. Yet he did not murmur, complain, fret, stew, or sit in a corner pouting. He knew that by the grace of God he was what he was. He knew that God had saved him in His time, not Paul's.

Paul also understood that grace is active. What God bestowed upon him would not go to waste; it would not be in vain. He would serve God with all of the grace God had given him.

This, Beloved, is my prayer for you and for me.

DAY FIVE

Those who are genuinely saved and who serve the Lord fall into two categories: those who serve out of "knowledge" and duty and those who serve out of a biblical understanding of the awareness of the unfathomable love and grace of God. If you watch carefully, you can spot the difference.

The first will hold rigidly to the law! They will be almost pharisaical in their Christianity, holding unwaveringly to standards, rules, or regulations, demanding much not only of themselves but of others. Many times they will struggle with God's unconditional love and acceptance. Their relationship with God will be performance-oriented. Whether God really loves them (and sometimes even others) will, in their estimation, depend upon whether or not they have "measured up."

Often they will keep people at arm's length, or they will attach themselves like a leech seeking love, security, approval, and a sense of worth from others. It's the only way they sense God's love for themselves. However, if the person pulls away or rejects them, they feel rejected by God. Serving God fulfills a need — theirs most of all.

What is the problem? Without trying to be all inclusive in my answer to this question, I would say the primary problem is that they do not understand and accept the grace of God. And when you don't understand the grace of God, it is difficult to understand His unconditional love.

People who do not understand or accept God's grace are often performance-oriented. In all probability, in the past their acceptance came on the basis of their performance — either because of the way they did something or because of what they produced. From this, they experienced a "pseudo" love. I say pseudo or false because it was a conditional love.

When they came to Christ, because their mind was not renewed or because they had knowledge of truth but did not comprehend the depth of His love and grace, it affected the way in which they served God. Wanting to please God, they served Him, which is commendable. However, not understanding the grace and love of God, they served Him in accordance with their "old" mind-set. And as I said before, but I believe it bears repeating so you won't miss it, they serve either under the legalism of the law or in order to have their own needs met. They feel that this is the way they gain purpose or worth. They do not understand that it is only "by the grace of God I am what I am." (In the next two days we'll cover this so that you are sure to understand it.)

My friend, have you faced what you are — what you were — or have you covered it up? If you do not allow love to uncover it and grace to heal it, you will continue to serve God in the wrong way.

Think about it, and we'll talk about it more tomorrow.

Day Six

"By the grace of God I am what I am" — do you really understand that statement? Let me seek to explain it to you. However, as I do, would you please take a moment to pray, asking our heavenly Father to open the eyes of your understanding to His truth and His truth alone?

Although you did not come to know God until a specific time, God knew you before the foundation of the world. Ephesians 1:4-5 says, "Just as He chose us in Him before the foundation of the world, that we should be holy and blameless before Him. **In love** He predestined us to adoption as sons through Jesus Christ to Himself."

What does this tell us? God is saying that He knows you — all about you. Before the foundation of the world He chose you.

"But surely God would not have chosen me because _____."

Because of what you have done? Because of what was done to you? Is that what you were going to say, my friend? Were you going to say that if God had known what you were — either by virtue of your own sin or by virtue of the sins of others perpetrated upon you — that He would not have chosen you?

You are wrong. God is **omniscient**. He knows everything. He's **omnipresent**. He was there when you did what you did. He was there when others did to you what they should not have done. God is your **Creator and the Sustainer** of your life. He knew what sperm would meet what egg to create you. And He is the **Righteous Judge**. He judged the sin of all mankind at the Cross when He put to death His Son as the sacrifice for the sins of all mankind. However, for those who will not accept this Sacrifice, risen from the dead, as their Lord and Savior, He will act as their personal Judge, for they have refused to be reconciled to God. They have chosen instead to continue as His enemy.

As you noticed, there are four things about God which I emphasized in bold print in the preceding paragraph. These are four truths taken from Psalm 139. This psalm is printed out for you. It contains truths that will liberate those who are held captive in the prison of their past. Therefore, I want you to take the time to go over this Psalm carefully. Don't skip over this wonderful assignment.

As you read, mark every reference to "God" including "Thou," "Thee," "Thy," "Thine." Mark each of these alike in a distinctive way. When you finish, make a list in the space at the end of the Psalm of everything you learn about God concerning His relationship to you.

Psalm 139 is divided into four stanzas of six verses each. I want you to write one of the four truths about God, which were printed in bold, over each stanza. Choose the one characteristic that best shows that particular aspect of God outlined in the stanza.

Psalm 139

1 O LORD, Thou hast searched me and known *me*.

2 Thou dost know when I sit down and when I rise up;

  Thou dost understand my thought from afar.

3 Thou dost scrutinize my path and my lying down,

  And art intimately acquainted with all my ways.

4 Even before there is a word on my tongue,

  Behold, O LORD, Thou dost know it all.

5 Thou hast enclosed me behind and before,

  And laid Thy hand upon me.

6 *Such* knowledge is too wonderful for me;

  It is *too* high, I cannot attain to it.

7 Where can I go from Thy Spirit?

  Or where can I flee from Thy presence?

8 If I ascend to heaven, Thou art there;

  If I make my bed in Sheol, behold, Thou art there.

9 If I take the wings of the dawn,

   If I dwell in the remotest part of the sea,

10 Even there Thy hand will lead me,

   And Thy right hand will lay hold of me.

11 If I say, "Surely the darkness will overwhelm me,

   And the light around me will be night,"

12 Even the darkness is not dark to Thee,

   And the night is as bright as the day.

   Darkness and light are alike *to Thee*.

13 For Thou didst form my inward parts;

   Thou didst weave me in my mother's womb.

14 I will give thanks to Thee, for I am fearfully and

     wonderfully made;

   Wonderful are Thy works,

   And my soul knows it very well.

15 My frame was not hidden from Thee,

   When I was made in secret,

   And skillfully wrought in the depths of the earth.

16 Thine eyes have seen my unformed substance;

And in Thy book they were all written,

The days that were ordained *for me*,

When as yet there was not one of them.

17 How precious also are Thy thoughts to me, O God!

How vast is the sum of them!

18 If I should count them, they would outnumber the sand.

When I awake, I am still with Thee.

19 O that Thou wouldst slay the wicked, O God;

Depart from me, therefore, men of bloodshed.

20 For they speak against Thee wickedly,

And Thine enemies take *Thy name* in vain.

21 Do I not hate those who hate Thee, O LORD?

And do I not loathe those who rise up against Thee?

22 I hate them with the utmost hatred;

They have become my enemies.

23 Search me, O God, and know my heart;

Try me and know my anxious thoughts;

24 And see if there be any hurtful way in me,

And lead me in the everlasting way.

DAY SEVEN

The man who wanted to kill Queen Elizabeth I did not succeed. However, God did not stop Paul in his plot to put many to death. Furiously enraged, Paul desired to rid the world of those of the Way who were polluting the Judaism he fiercely served.

Paul, who was then named Saul, watched Stephen collapse under the relentless plummeting of the stones. But he heard Stephen's last words, "Lord, do not hold this sin against them!" (Acts 7:60). Although Stephen's bloody and noble death did not stop Paul from continuing his great persecution of these "Christians," it did nag at his conscience. He continued to murder many, but it became increasingly hard to "kick against the goads" (Acts 26:14).

When the grace of God catapulted Paul to the ground as he set out for Damascus in pursuit of his despised enemies, the warrings of Paul's conscience came to an end. However, he still had to deal with reality. He had been a murderer, not of the wicked but of those who followed the Christ Who now spoke to him. "'Saul, Saul, why are you persecuting Me? It is hard for you to kick against the goads.' And I said, 'Who art Thou, Lord?' And the Lord said, 'I am Jesus whom you are persecuting. But arise, and stand on your feet; for this purpose I have appeared to you, to appoint you a minister and a witness not only to the things which you have seen, but also to the things in which I will appear to you; delivering you from the *Jewish* people and from the Gentiles, to whom I am sending you, to open their eyes so that they may turn from darkness to light and from the dominion of Satan to God, in order that they may receive forgiveness of sins and an inheritance among those who have been sanctified by faith in Me'" (Acts 26:14b-18).

How did Paul deal with his sin? You know the answer, don't you?! He dealt with it by understanding and accepting the grace of God. Paul never hid, buried, or denied his past. He dealt with it. That, Beloved, is why Paul could serve God the way he served Him and say, "By the grace of God I am what I am."

Was it because Paul understood, accepted, and lived in the light of the grace of God that he became the teacher of grace for the New Testament? I think possibly so.

My friend, what do you know of the grace of God? Do you live in the light of His grace? Are your dealings with others on the basis of God's grace? Or do you slip back into law because that is where you live? I plead with you. Let love uncover your past, and let the balm of grace heal it. God, in His omniscience and sovereignty, allowed you to experience what you experienced. His intent was not to destroy you, for His thoughts toward you are precious. Rather, His purpose was to use it all to mold and to make you into His child, a child upon whom He would delight to pour out His love. A child who would serve Him in the fullness of His grace.

What needs to be uncovered, dealt with, healed by His grace?[1] Write it out.

Remember that your heavenly Father loves you with an everlasting love. And the plans He has for you are for good, not evil, to give you a future and a hope (Jeremiah 31:3; 29:11).

Chapter 7, Notes

[1]If you continue to have a difficult time dealing with your hurts, may I suggest that you purchase my devotional study *Lord, Heal My Hurts*? There are audio and video tapes which accompany this study, but I would suggest that you not listen to the tapes without doing the study yourself. It will not be as effective if you do not get into God's healing Word yourself. Using *Lord, Heal My Hurts* will get you into the Word. God has used this study in such an incredible way in ministering His healing to so many. You may contact our offices at Precept Ministries to obtain this study.

As each one has received a special gift, employ it in serving one another, as good stewards of the manifold grace of God.

I Peter 4:10

Grace?
The Power for
Ministry?

DAY ONE

It does not matter who you have been or what you have done because the grace of God will enable you to be all that you should be. By the grace of God you are what you are. However, grace does not stop there. Although grace is freely given, by the very nature of its power grace confronts its recipients with an obligation — the obligation to allow God's grace to be manifested through them.

Grace provides us with everything that is Christ's, for it makes us heirs of God and joint-heirs with our Lord Jesus Christ. Consequently, grace does not leave man inert or impotent. Grace is not inactive. This is why Paul says, "But by the grace of God I am what I am, and His grace toward me did not prove vain; but I labored even more than all of them, yet not I, but the grace of God with me" (I Corinthians 15:10). In Philippians 2:13 we saw that it is God Who is at work in us both to will and to do of His good pleasure. Ours is to say, "Jesus, be Jesus in me," as the song puts it, and to let His grace manifest itself as we reach out to others. Jesus is able to be "Jesus in you" because of the indwelling presence of the Holy Spirit.

The book of Acts is an account of what happened when the Holy Spirit came to indwell believers. The grace and truth realized in Christ Jesus has continued down through the centuries as God's children have carried out to completion that which God was working in them by allowing the grace of God to labor through their lives.

When the Apostles wanted to know when Jesus would restore the kingdom to Israel, i.e., when God's Kingdom would be set up on earth as had been promised in Daniel Chapter 7 and in other Old Testament passages, Jesus replied, "It is not for you to know times or epochs which the Father has fixed by His own authority; but you shall receive power when the Holy Spirit has come upon you; and you shall be My witnesses both in Jerusalem, and in all Judea and Samaria, and even to the remotest part of the earth" (Acts 1:7-8).

They were looking for the Kingdom; Jesus was telling them to occupy until He comes! One of the problems in Christendom today is that we have become occupied with trying to discern when He is coming instead of focusing on our responsibility to be about our Father's business, laboring in His grace so that we will not be ashamed when He comes.

Failure to allow His grace to labor through us when it is available to us in all of its power — this will be our greatest regret, our greatest shame.

Day Two

This week I want to look at several principles which I believe will greatly help you so that someday you can say with Paul that God's grace was not poured out on you in vain.

First, Paul knew that we have access to the grace of God through faith in Jesus Christ. This is clearly stated in Romans 5:2.

1. Write out Romans 5:1-2.

The verb "stand" in the statement "in which we stand" is in the perfect tense. In Greek the perfect tense indicates that it is an action which took place in the past but which continues to be true. Thus, at salvation you and I were not only given access to the grace of God for that particular moment, but we stand there **right now**. Having access to the grace of God means that everything Jesus Christ is and everything He has is made available to you. The power of grace rests upon you.

This is why Peter exhorts the recipients of his first epistle the way he does.

2. Write out I Peter 5:12.

3. What is Peter exhorting his readers to do with respect to grace?

In the opening of his epistle, he wrote, "May grace and peace be yours in fullest measure" (I Peter 1:2b). He wants them to make sure that they do not fail of the grace of God. It is one thing to have access to God's grace; it is another thing to appropriate it. Peter wrote his epistle to people who needed to understand suffering and, in the midst of their suffering, to remember how to relate to others — to those outside the faith, to those in positions of political power, to the elders of the church. He dealt with them on the relationship of slaves and masters, husbands and wives, the young and the old. Appropriating the grace of God in its fullest measure would enable them to serve God in an acceptable way.

To have the grace of God to serve Him in an acceptable way but not to stand firm in that grace and use it to its fullest is to have God's grace poured out on you in vain.

Think about it. Are you in a difficult relationship? God's grace is there. You have access to it. Allow Him to control you rather than being controlled by the circumstances of that relationship.

Are you frustrated with the governmental powers? Do you want to rebel? There is grace to enable you to "submit yourselves for the Lord's sake to every human institution" (I Peter 2:13).

Are you living with an unsaved and difficult husband? There is grace to enable you to be submissive to your own husband so that even if he is disobedient to the Word he may be won without a word by observing your chaste and respectful behavior as you adorn yourself in the hidden person of your heart with a gentle and quiet spirit. There is grace to enable you to respond as Christ responded to those who mistreated Him (I Peter 2:21-3:6).

As a husband, are you frustrated with your wife, unable to understand her? There is grace to enable you to live with her in an understanding way and to honor her as you should (I Peter 3:7).

Are you being reviled by others because of your Christianity? There is grace to enable you to endure without returning insult for insult, evil for evil (I Peter 3:8-4:19).

Is spiritual warfare wearing you down? Are you weary in battle? There is grace to enable you to resist. "And after you have suffered for a little while, the God of all grace, who called you to His eternal glory in Christ, will Himself perfect, confirm, strengthen *and* establish you" (I Peter 5:10).

To stand firm in the grace of God is to serve God rather than serving self. Acceptable service unto God is manifesting His grace by the way in which you live. Therefore, keep in mind this first principle: **The child of God always has access to the grace of God; therefore, stand firm in it.**

DAY THREE

There is a second principle of which you need to be cognizant: **The grace of God provides you with spiritual gifts by which you are to serve the Body of Jesus Christ.**

As a steward of these gifts, you will be held accountable for using them.

Let's take a brief look at what the New Testament teaches on the subject of spiritual gifts. Look up the following verses and write out what you learn from each with respect to spiritual gifts. Each time you see the word "grace" in any of these verses, you may want to mark it in a distinctive way in your Bible. (I color "grace" blue [a heavenly color] and circle it with yellow [because He is the light]. Then, I can spot it immediately when I study or teach.)

1. Ephesians 4:7-8

2. I Corinthians 12:4-7

3. I Corinthians 12:11 (Considering what you saw in verses 4-7, record what is distributed.)

4. Romans 12:6

5. I Peter 4:10-11

Now write out a summary statement of what you have learned about spiritual gifts.

How does what you have learned fit with the second principle I gave you at the beginning of today's devotional study?

DAY FOUR

The grace of God puts us into God's forever family, and it is within the family that each is to serve God according to the measure of His grace. You have seen that every believer has been given one or more spiritual gifts. These gifts are not given according to merit or man's desire. Rather "God has placed the members, each one of them, in the body, just as He desired" (I Corinthians 12:18).

When we received the Lord Jesus Christ, "by one Spirit we were all baptized into one body, . . . and we were all made to drink of one Spirit" (I Corinthians 12:13). When this happens, it is God Who determines where we are placed in the Body.

Every time God deals with the subject of spiritual gifts, He uses the analogy of the body. This is because the body is one entity. Yet its members are diverse and function in unique ways for the proper working of the whole. Its various members illustrate what the Church of Jesus Christ is all about — unity in the midst of diversity all under the headship of Jesus Christ.

As you saw in I Corinthians 12:4-7, the gifts, the ministries, and even the effects are all from the Godhead. God supplies us with everything we need in order to do what He has called us to do. This, my friend, is all of grace. Our gifts "differ according to the grace given to us" (Romans 12:6). And we are given grace "according to the measure of Christ's gift" (Ephesians 4:7).

And how does all of this fit into our study of grace — grace that is active and labors? It is concisely stated in I Peter 4:10: "As each one has received a *special* gift, employ it in serving one another, as good stewards of the manifold grace of God."

Have you ever realized that God, in His grace, has gifted you in a very special and unique way so that you might serve Him? I remember the first time I learned this. I was writing a course on the book of Romans, and I came to Romans 12:4-8. There I saw that we were to stay within the sphere of our gift: "Or ministry, *let us wait* on *our* ministering" (KJV).

My mouth dropped open, for suddenly I realized that I couldn't stay within the realm of my gift if I did not know what my gift was. That began my personal study of the whole subject of spiritual gifts. I didn't run to books about spiritual gifts. I turned to a thorough topical study of the subject from the Bible. What I learned became our *Precept Upon Precept* course on spiritual gifts.[1]

May I urge you to think about these things. God not only calls you to serve Him, but He gifts you so that you can.

DAY FIVE

I believe that one of the things which made the Apostle Paul such an effective instrument in the hands of God was that Paul knew exactly what God had gifted him to do. He knew it, and he served God and the Body of Jesus Christ within the framework of his gifts. Thus, the grace of God labored through him.

When Paul was imprisoned in Rome the first time, he wrote to the church at Ephesus, stating that the stewardship of God's grace had been given to him for them as Gentiles. With that stewardship came a ministry and the power to perform that ministry. Watch for the words "grace," "minister," and "power" in Ephesians 3:7-8, which is printed out for you, and underline them.

Ephesians 3:7-8

7 of which I was made a minister, according to the gift

of God's grace which was given to me according to the

working of His power.

8 To me, the very least of all saints, this grace was given,

to preach to the Gentiles the unfathomable riches of

Christ,

In Romans 1:4-5 Paul writes, "Jesus Christ our Lord, through whom we have received grace and apostleship to bring about *the* obedience of faith among all the Gentiles, for His name's sake." Paul realized that in the grace of God he had been called to be an apostle. It didn't matter to him that he was "the least of the apostles." He would not refuse to serve God if he could not be foremost. Instead, he would appropriate God's grace to the fullest. There would not be one measure of grace that Paul would not use up.

This brings us to the third principle you need to remember so that God's grace is not poured out on you in vain: **With the grace of God comes a specific purpose for your life.** Ephesians 2:8-10 says, "For by grace you have been saved through faith; and that not of yourselves, *it is* the gift of God; not as a result of works, that no one should boast. For we are His workmanship, created in Christ Jesus for good works, which God prepared beforehand, that we should walk in them."

1. In the light of these verses, what do you learn regarding the purpose for your life?

2. How would you tie these verses in with what you learned about spiritual gifts?

When Paul knew his ministry on earth was coming to a close, he wrote Timothy, his son in the gospel, his final letter. In that letter Paul exhorts Timothy to kindle afresh the gift of God which is in him, reminding Timothy that God has not given us a spirit of timidity, but of power and love and discipline. "Therefore do not be ashamed of the testimony of our Lord, or of me His prisoner; but join with *me* in suffering for the gospel according to the power of God, who has saved us, and called us with a holy calling, not according to our works, but according to His own purpose and grace which was granted us in Christ Jesus from all eternity" (II Timothy 1:8-9).

3. As you read these verses, what do you learn about the calling of God in a Christian's life?

In II Timothy 1:11-12, Paul writes: "For which I was appointed a preacher and an apostle and a teacher. For this reason I also suffer these things, but I am not ashamed; for I know whom I have believed and I am convinced that He is able to guard what I have entrusted to Him until that day."

4. What had God in grace appointed Paul to do?

5. According to these verses, why was Paul able to serve God even though he suffered?

6. Are you able to do the same, even though you suffer? Why?

7. If Paul hadn't served God even though he suffered, what would that tell you about Paul's attitude or response to the grace of God?

8. Beloved, what has been your response to the grace of God?

DAY SIX

If God's grace is not to be poured out on you in vain, the fourth and final principle of grace by which you must live is **faith**. It is one thing to stand in the grace of God and to be gifted by God for the work of ministry. It is another thing to live in the light of these facts. This is where faith comes in. Faith activates or releases the grace of God.

Grace strips all men of their need of anything but humility. Then, it gives to the humble a vault of all the treasures and resources of God. However, that vault is only unlocked with the key of faith. This is why there is such impotence in the lives of many of God's children.

First, they have not humbled themselves under the mighty hand of God. Instead, they have listened to and brought into the pulpit messages and books which exalt man. They have been seduced into a "pseudo" faith which centers on what we believe about ourselves and our own human potential and capability.

Second, they do not understand biblical faith. Their faith is placed on what they believe about God rather than on what the **whole counsel of the Word of God** has to say. The certainty of faith is found not in the believer but in who and what is believed. If we believe in what we say, our faith rests in ourselves. If we believe what God says — **in the context of the whole Bible** — our faith rests in the infallible Word of God and in the character of God. "For Thou hast magnified Thy word according to all Thy name" (Psalm 138:2b). "According to" can be translated "together with." God is saying that if the Word fails, His name fails. Therefore, the Word of God stands because God stands by His Word.

Have you trusted in that Word?

DAY SEVEN

If you are going to serve God in the power and strength of grace, you must take Him at His Word. Let me say it again so that you don't miss it: Grace strips all men of their need of anything but humility, and grace opens to the humble a vault of all the treasures and resources of God which we unlock with the key of faith. Grace and faith cannot be separated. You cannot lay hold of grace apart from faith.

By faith we totally rely on God, rejecting confidence in ourselves and placing our confidence in Who God is and in what He says. This is how we are to live in every situation of life. Think with me for a moment, and you will see what I mean.

When we sin as a child of God, what makes us right with God? Must we do penance? Sacrifice something? Promise that we will never do it again? You know the verse already. God says, "If we confess our sins, He is faithful and righteous to forgive us our sins and to cleanse us from all unrighteousness" (I John 1:9). How can God do this? Grace. Yet, what releases this grace? Faith that acts on what God says in I John 1:9. If you don't handle your sin God's way, it will affect your service for God.

When you encounter various sorts of trials that you feel will overwhelm or destroy you, how can you survive without losing your faith or your mind? You must believe God that His grace is sufficient for any and every circumstance of life. The minute you believe, the power of grace is released. All of this is taught in II Corinthians Chapter 12, and we will look at it in depth in our final week of study. Just remember that if you do not appropriate in faith God's all-sufficient grace in the trials of life, it will affect your service for God. Without appropriating His grace, your trials can overwhelm you or consume your thoughts, thereby, distracting you from God's calling upon your life.

When you encounter what seems to be failure and you feel that there is no going on, no way to recover your mistakes, what will keep you from drowning in the quicksand of despair? What will keep you from bitterness, anger, lashing out? Faith in the grace of God which promises that all things will work together for good. If you do not appropriate this promise in faith and rely on God's abounding grace, your failures will keep you from going forward in service for Him.

O Beloved, do you see that it is one thing to have access to the grace of God but that it is another thing to appropriate it? Notice that I said "appropriate." Grace can never be earned or merited. It can only be believed, appropriated by faith. *"The* righteousness of God is revealed from faith to faith; as it is written, 'BUT THE RIGHTEOUS *man* SHALL LIVE BY FAITH'" (Romans 1:17). The Christian life begins with faith, is lived by faith, and is maintained by faith. It is all of faith.

"Therefore, since we receive a kingdom which cannot be shaken, let us show gratitude, by which we may offer to God **an acceptable service** with reverence and awe" (Hebrews 12:28).

Chapter 8, Notes

[1]God has used that course to liberate and activate many Christians as they discovered what God, by His grace, had gifted them to do. If you are interested in this study on Spiritual Gifts, you should contact our offices at Precept Ministries.

And after you have suffered for a little while, the God of all grace, who called you to His eternal glory in Christ, will Himself perfect, confirm, strengthen and establish you.

I Peter 5:10

Grace?
Sufficient for My
Sufferings & Trials?

DAY ONE

Having been justified by faith, you have "peace with God through our Lord Jesus Christ, through whom also we have obtained our introduction by faith into this grace in which we stand" (Romans 5:1-2). As you stand firm in the grace of God, you will find it sufficient for every situation of life. This is the subject of our final week of study: **the sufficiency of God's grace no matter how difficult the situation.**

In one of the most difficult and trying times of Paul's life, he received the greatest blessing. And yet, the blessing, awesome though it was, led again to another trial of

177

his faith. If we live sold-out lives for our Lord, we can know for certain that our lives will never be without suffering. "And indeed, all who desire to live godly in Christ Jesus will be persecuted" (II Timothy 3:12).

This is exactly what happened to Paul. What encouragement we can find in his life! At one time "Jews came from Antioch and Iconium, and having won over the multitudes, they stoned Paul and dragged him out of the city, supposing him to be dead" (Acts 14:19).

It could have been this awful persecution which led to one of the most awesome experiences in his life. In II Corinthians Chapter 12 in the midst of defending himself and his ministry to his Corinthian children, Paul wrote the following:

II Corinthians 12:2-10

I know a man in Christ who fourteen years ago — whether in the body I do not know, or out of the body I do not know, God knows — such a man was caught up to the third heaven. And I know how such a man — whether in the body or apart from the body I do not know, God knows — was caught up into Paradise, and heard inexpressible words, which a man is not permitted to speak. On behalf of such a man will I boast; but on my own behalf I will not boast, except in regard to *my* weaknesses. For if I do wish to boast I shall not be foolish, for I shall be speaking the truth; but I refrain *from this*, so that no one may credit me with more than he sees *in* me or hears from me. And because of the surpassing greatness of the revelations, for this reason, to keep me from exalting myself, there was given me a thorn in the flesh, a messenger of Satan to buffet me — to keep me from exalting myself! Concerning this I entreated the Lord three times that it might depart from me. And He has said to me, "My grace is sufficient for you, for power is perfected in weakness." Most gladly, therefore, I will rather boast about my weaknesses, that the power of Christ may dwell in me. Therefore I am well content with weaknesses, with insults, with distresses, with persecutions, with difficulties, for Christ's sake; for when I am weak, then I am strong.

1. Where was Paul caught up to? It is described in two ways. Please note both.

2. What do you see in the fact that Paul would not talk about or boast about what happened to him when he was caught up to God?

3. What happened to Paul as a result of the revelations God allowed him to have? Why?

4. What did Paul ask God to do, and how did God respond?

5. What did you learn about the grace of God from this passage?

6. Can you see how you could apply this passage to your own life? How?

DAY TWO

Grace does not exempt us from trials; it takes us through them. No matter what you are suffering, dear child of God, God's grace is sufficient. This is the message of II Corinthians 12:1-10.

Three times Paul went to God beseeching Him to remove the thorn in his flesh. What that thorn was we do not know, for he does not tell us. We do know that it was in his flesh, that it was a messenger of Satan to buffet him, and that it was allowed by God to keep Paul from exalting himself. Paul knew that the thorn came filtered through God's sovereign fingers of love. Satan brought it; God allowed it. Therefore, Paul went to God on three separate occasions, asking Him to remove it.

The third time God gave Paul His answer — an answer never to be contested again, an answer Paul was to live with for the rest of his life. Paul writes, "Concerning this I entreated the Lord three times that it might depart from me. And He has said to me. . . ." "Has said" is in the perfect tense, which, as I said before, is a past completed action with a present or continuing result. Thus, "has said" means in essence, "This is My answer; don't ask again."

How would Paul endure this torment, this suffering? The same way any child of God is to live through (Notice that I said "through.") suffering or trials, no matter how short or long their duration — **by God's all-sufficient grace!**

If God's grace were not sufficient, the trial could not happen. God has given us a wonderful promise which we need to keep ever before us in times of difficulty. Interestingly enough, He also gave it to the Corinthians through Paul: "No temptation has overtaken you but such as is common to man; and God is faithful, who will not allow you to be tempted beyond what you are able, but with the temptation will provide the way of escape also, that you may be able to endure it" (I Corinthians 10:13).

Therefore, Beloved, **when you suffer you must remember** the following: **First, it is not more than you can bear.**

Second, God has a way of escape. However, that way of escape is not to run from the trial or circumstance. You must take God's way of escape, not yours. Today so many have such an unbiblical concept of trials, suffering, and God. They cannot imagine a God of love allowing one of His children to suffer. To think in this way is to show one's ignorance of the whole counsel of God.

It is given to us not only to believe on Jesus Christ, but to suffer for His name's sake (Philippians 1:29-30). God uses trials to bring us to Christlike maturity. Everywhere trials are discussed, from Romans Chapter 5 to James Chapter 1 to I Peter Chapter 1, you see this message. In each of these incidents we are told to endure, to abide under — to *hupomenō* as the Greek puts it.

Therefore, when you look to God for "the way of escape," make sure that it is **His** way of escape, not your way or your rationalization of His way. He will hold you accountable.

Third, His grace is sufficient. Why is it sufficient? Because, as I have said before, grace is not inactive. It is not merely a creed to be quoted. It is power which is to be appropriated in faith. Watch how Paul expresses it and connects power with grace: "And He has said to me, 'My grace is sufficient for you, for power is perfected in weakness.' Most gladly, therefore, I will rather boast about my weaknesses, that the power of Christ may dwell in me" (II Corinthians 12:9). "Dwell" means "to abide in, be at home in."

1. Mark "power" and "grace" in those two sentences. Can you see how they are synonymous? How?

In the next verse Paul writes, "Therefore I am well content with weaknesses, with insults, with distresses, with persecutions, with difficulties, for Christ's sake; for when I am weak, then I am strong" (II Corinthians 12:10).

2. Why is Paul strong when he is weak?

3. Considering verses 9 and 10, why would Paul boast in these things?

It is one thing to grit your teeth, to bear your trials, and through those clenched teeth to say, "Well, I guess His grace'll be sufficient." It is another thing to say, "I am well content with weaknesses, insults, distresses, persecutions, and difficulties." When you say the latter, you prove that you know that His grace is sufficient.

My friend, where do you stand? Where do you want to stand? Can you? Why? How?

DAY THREE

How often we would love to mount up with wings as eagles and soar above our problems and distresses, leaving them below as we glide effortlessly high above it all. And yet, many times grace lets us plod, or should I say just keep persevering, rather than soaring blissfully above it all. Such was the life of William Carey, a cobbler turned missionary.

At an old age, after enduring great and plentiful hardships, he wrote:
"If anyone should think it worth his while to write my life, if he give me credit for being a plodder he will describe me justly. I can plod. I

can persevere in any definite pursuit. To this I owe everything."[1]

Grace enabled Carey to plod. It was William Carey who coined the phrase that has endured since the late 1700's, echoing over and over again the sufficiency and power of God's grace: "Expect great things *from* God. Attempt great things *for* God."[2]

These words were preached to lethargic Christian leaders, ministers of the gospel, who had ignored and then forgotten the commission of their Christ to go into all the world and preach the gospel to every creature. Into his sermon Carey "poured all the longings of his heart for the past eight years. Over and over he repeated the phrase [Expect great things from God. Attempt great things for God.] until it sank into the hearts of those who heard. The words came from the soul of the preacher and spread across his listeners with the impact of an explosion. They were jolted out of their lethargy as the Holy Spirit moved among them. It was the era of long and ponderous sermons, but this time the address was short and simple. This was a burning bush of missionary enterprise, calling to the listless churches of the day to enlarge their tents, to lengthen their self-centered cords, to widen their vision.

"Carey told them: 'God is calling you to a brilliant future, to preach the gospel throughout the world. My friends, you need this wider vision.'"[3] They needed it. But for years, only he would heed it. The question of his listeners was, "What can a mere handful of preachers accomplish?" They had failed to consider the grace of God — power for service that takes mere man and accomplishes the work of God through him!

Do you still wonder the same? Put it away; file your doubts and your impotence under the grace of God. If you cannot soar with eagle's wings, plod on in faith.

The souls of the men who listened to Carey's message were stirred, but they were not moved to any action beyond a resolution to come up with a plan for sending missionaries to regions beyond the shores of England.

It was a resolution to make a plan. That was as far as it went until Carey plodded on in the grace of God, formulating the plan himself. A year later at their annual October gathering he unfolded his plan, and "The Particular Baptist Society for the Propagation of the Gospel amongst the Heathen" came into being through the just-formed Missionary Society. William Carey would be their first missionary, but not without great cost.

Very little was known of India and her way of life, and it was fifteen thousand danger-ridden miles away.

Carey thought about how, since their marriage, he had taught Dorothy to read. The task had needed all the patience he could muster for she did not find learning an easy task. Could she now be willing to go and live among people who could not even speak to her in that same language? He reflected that it was he who had built the altar and for himself there was no thought of turning away, but how right was it to ask his wife to share in the sacrifice? To go without her would mean death to his happiness, but if that were the only alternative, then so be it.

It was nearly morning when William reached home, cold as stone, desperately hungry and thirsty. Very soon Dorothy had the kettle boiling on the hob. As they sat drinking their hot tea Carey told his wife of his plans.

'Go to India?' she gasped. 'No, William, never!'

She looked at him with bewildered eyes. Leave their little home and everyone they knew? It was unthinkable.

'We cannot go, William! We have our children to think of. There is your church here, and your home. Surely God wouldn't want you to leave everything?'

'My dear, you don't understand. I know God has asked me to go to India for him. He has called me. I have answered and I cannot draw back. I would not if I could,' replied William, urgently, willing her to understand.

But Dorothy was adamant. Fuller and Sutcliff heard that she refused to go to India so they travelled to Leicester to try to persuade her to change her mind. It was of no use and she declared that if William must go, then she would remain here with her children and prepare herself for the parting.

Carey was grieved beyond telling and but for his firm faith and devotion to Christ he might even yet have given up the project. However, during the following week he wrote to his father at Paulerspury: '. . . I hope, dear father, you may be enabled to surrender me up to the Lord for the most arduous, honourable, and important work that ever any of the sons of men were called to engage in. I have many sacrifices to make. I must part with a beloved family and a number of most affectionate friends. . . . But I have set my hand to the plough.'

'Is William mad?' shouted his father when he read the letter.

The following Sunday William broke the news to his large congregation at Harvey Lane. At first they were dumb with grief at the thought of losing such a pastor whose faithful ministry had been a source of such blessing. Some even refused to give him up, maintaining that it was not right for him to leave a work when God was using his ministry so remarkably.

But gradually they came to see that this was in fact God answering their prayer for the spread of Christ's kingdom among the heathen, and that he was asking them to join in the first sacrifice. When they realized this they were not only prepared to let him go, but were ready to back him in every way possible, rejoicing in the fact that they were the church that was sending him. Even so, they wrote in the church minute book: 'Though it is at the expense of losing one whom we love as our own souls.'

In the end it was arranged that Carey should take his eldest son, Felix, with him to India, and return in a year or two for his wife and the other children.

No other cause would have made him give up his family and he did not falter. Only if God himself provided a 'ram in the thicket', as he did for Abraham, could there be any deviation in the sacrifice.[4]

There was no way to soar, but Carey would plod on in God's all-sufficient grace, and the power of God would rest upon him.

DAY FOUR

It was the grace of God which held Carey when the cost of his trip seemed impossible to raise, when the pain of the impending separation from his wife and children pierced his heart, when it became difficult to find a captain of a ship who would take him as a passenger.

The East India Company did not want missionaries spoiling their business by proclaiming the gospel to the heathens. There was delay after delay as promises were broken and captains were intimidated. Thomas, a man who had lived in India and wanted to return as a missionary under their Society, was to travel with Carey.

While Thomas was away the captain of the *Earl of Oxford* developed 'cold feet' about his offer to take the missionaries without the East India Company's leave. The risk suddenly appeared too great. He would take Mrs Thomas and her daughter but finally refused to take the others.

Moved almost to tears as he watched the ship disappearing over the skyline, Carey's heart was in a tumult. What was God doing to him? Was this to be the ignominious end of all his hopes to reach India? He was indeed downcast, but not in complete despair. God was moving in mysterious ways but his wonders would be, must be, brought to pass. His servants must go on expecting the great things that had been promised.

Carey . . . returned to Portsmouth and took the coach to London. There was news from home that the expected baby had arrived and he now had another son. He had written to his wife: 'If I had all the world I would freely give it all to have you

and the children with me.' With this unexpected change of plan there might be an opportunity to see them all once more.

[Carey, Felix, and Thomas] heard that a Danish boat, the *Kron Princessa Maria*, was on her way from Copenhagen and expected shortly. They learnt that the fare for the three of them would be £250. All they had was the sum refunded by the captain of the *Earl of Oxford*, £150, but in faith they booked their passage.

Then, like a couple of excited schoolboys suddenly released from lessons, they dashed off to Piddington to see the family again before the Danish ship would be ready to sail.

When William lifted the latch of the cottage door and walked in, it was no wonder Dorothy looked, gasped, and burst into tears. She was dreaming. She must be. A dream that was too good to be true! Then surprise gave place to delight and eagerly she fetched the new baby to meet his father.

As her sister Katherine prepared a hurried breakfast for them all, Carey took the opportunity to appeal to his wife once more to change her mind and go with him to India. They prayed together over the matter but still Dorothy was too afraid to take what seemed to be such a dangerous step into the dark.

When the time came to say goodbye the two men ... set out. ... Carey was so overcome with grief at the parting that after a few miles Thomas, whose sympathetic nature could not bear to see it, decided they must return and make one more effort.

Dorothy's loving heart could stand no more, and in tears she said she would go if her sister would go too. Taken aback by this sudden turn of events, Katherine had only a few minutes to make up her mind. She sent up a quick prayer for guidance.

Early in the morning of June 13th, 1793, the whole family went aboard the sailing ship *Kron Princessa Maria* and all hundred and thirty feet of her length seemed to Carey as pure gold. This was the ship that was to take not only himself, but his wife and children, across the vast ocean to an unknown land. He was at last on his way to a people he already loved because of their need, and to a work that was dearer to him than life itself.

The England that had given him birth, and taught him much of life and its meaning, became smaller as he and Dorothy stood on deck and watched its coastline grow blurred, before passing for ever from their view. They never returned to this country.[5]

Upon arriving in India, Carey encountered one trial after another. His money dwindled because Thomas spent their whole year's allowance in their first ten weeks in India. His missionary efforts were violently opposed and threatened by the government. He sought some means of employment and housing for his homeless family already plagued with dysentery and homesickness.

As Carey reviewed his life during these days of trial it looked as if circumstances had indeed torn

it into worthless fragments. As yet he was not able to see these shreds through God's kaleidoscope where every piece fitted to make a perfect pattern. A movement of the hand holding the instrument was sufficient to change the pattern but this did not mar it or dull its beauty. Gradually he came to realize this and even as he brooded, something of the peace of God came through to him.

When he was offered a piece of land at Debhatta in the Sunderbans, with the possibility of being able to use the bungalow belonging to the Salt Department, he accepted it, together with the cobras and tigers he knew lived in the forests round about. He claimed the promise of God for protection from these dangers.[6]

Little did this missionary realize that it would be seven years before he would see his first Indian saved by the grace of God and then undergo great persecution from his people. On that day Dorothy did not stand at his side; she was confined to her room, mentally ill. This Carey did not realize either. All he knew was that God's grace is sufficient and that His power is perfected in our weakness.

He would need to know this, to ever remember it, for eleven years of mission work would take the lives of seven of his co-laborers who followed him to India, including Thomas. For the next twenty-three years, only three of them would be left to carry on the work "as a three-fold cord, each depending on the others and drawing strength from that fellowship. They became known as the 'Serampore Triad.'"[7]

Carey again found God's grace sufficient when, in 1812, tragedy struck and fire destroyed the Serampore

Press along with much of Carey's translation work. He wrote:

> 'The loss is heavy, but as travelling the road a second time, however painful it may be, is usually done with greater ease and certainty, so I trust the work will lose nothing in real value. . . . The work is already begun again in every language.'[8]

In 1833 fever and weakness caused him to be confined to a chair placed on two boards and rolled around on four wheels, and then the day came when he was confined to his home. Still, this harvester of grace plodded on, going over the final proofs of his Bengali New Testament.

Then, "as the sun rose into a cloudless sky on the morning of June 9th, 1834, the pioneer reached the last rung of the ladder. As he entered into the eternal presence of the Author, in his hand was the new edition of the Bengali New Testament.

"India had said goodbye to one of her greatest benefactors, and on the Danish Government House at Serampore the flag was seen to be flying at half-mast."[9]

Once when some visitors came to see Carey, then confined to his room, one of the men spoke glowingly of Carey's accomplishments. When the time came for the man to leave, Carey said softly, "Mr. Duff, you have been talking much of Dr. Carey. When I am gone, say nothing about Carey. Speak instead of Carey's Saviour."[10]

"But by the grace of God I am what I am, and His grace toward me did not prove vain. . ." (I Corinthians 15:10).

O Father, may Your grace in my life not be in vain. May I ever draw from its sufficiency, and may I ever serve You in its power. I pray this for myself and for those for whom I labor in writing this study. I ask it all through the grace given to me in Your Son, my Lord and Saviour Jesus Christ.

DAY FIVE

When things don't go our way, when our happiness is threatened by the trials of life, when God isn't giving us what we want, when seemingly our needs are not being met, there is a great temptation to take our way out, to turn back to our old ways, to yield to our flesh, or to give up in discouragement.

This is what was happening to the recipients of the letter to the Hebrews. They didn't understand that the trials they were enduring were part of God's discipline. And so in the eleventh chapter of his word of exhortation, the author of Hebrews reminds them of their need of faith. Things are not over; the drama of redemption has not yet come to an end. If they want God's approval, they must continue in faith.

"Now faith is the assurance of *things* hoped for, the conviction of things not seen. For by it the men of old gained approval." And with that introduction, the author reminded them of the men of old and their walk of faith — faith that endured although they "did not receive what was promised" (Hebrews 11:1-2, 39).

Then, pointing back to the "so great a cloud of witnesses," he exhorted them to "lay aside every encumbrance, and the sin which so easily entangles us, and . . . run with endurance the race that is set before us, fixing our eyes on Jesus, the author and perfecter of faith, who for the joy set before Him endured the cross, despising the shame, and has sat down at the right hand of the throne of God" (Hebrews 12:1-2). What they were encountering was known by God. It was His discipline to further refine them, to free them from encumbrances and sins which were keeping them from His likeness. Once again he directed them to look to the throne.

Throughout the pages of this exquisite letter to the Hebrews, we are constantly reminded that we have access to God's throne of grace. Jesus, our Great High Priest, has passed through the heavens. Therefore, we must hold fast our confession and "draw near with confidence to the throne of grace, that we may receive mercy and may find grace to help in time of need" (Hebrews 4:16).

Like you and me, they needed to remember that grace does not exempt us from suffering and trials but that it sees us through them. Our responsibility is to avail ourselves of the grace which flows from His throne.

In their suffering and trials, he gives them the following reminder:

Hebrews 12:5-17

5 and you have forgotten the exhortation which is addressed to you as sons,

"MY SON, DO NOT REGARD LIGHTLY THE DISCIPLINE OF THE

LORD,

NOR FAINT WHEN YOU ARE REPROVED BY HIM;

6 FOR THOSE WHOM THE LORD LOVES HE DISCIPLINES,

AND HE SCOURGES EVERY SON WHOM HE RECEIVES."

7 It is for discipline that you endure; God deals with you as with sons; for what son is there whom *his* father does not discipline?

8 But if you are without discipline, of which all have become partakers, then you are illegitimate children and not sons.

9 Furthermore, we had earthly fathers to discipline us, and we respected them; shall we not much rather be subject to the Father of spirits, and live?

10 For they disciplined us for a short time as seemed best to them, but He disciplines us for *our* good, that we may share His holiness.

11 All discipline for the moment seems not to be joyful, but sorrowful; yet to those who have been trained by it, afterwards it yields the peaceful fruit of righteousness.

12 Therefore, strengthen the hands that are weak and the knees that are feeble,

13 and make straight paths for your feet, so that *the limb*

which is lame may not be put out of joint, but rather be

healed.

14 Pursue peace with all men, and the sanctification

without which no one will see the Lord.

15 See to it that no one comes short of the grace of God;

that no root of bitterness springing up causes trouble,

and by it many be defiled;

16 that *there be* no immoral or godless person like Esau,

who sold his own birthright for a *single* meal.

17 For you know that even afterwards, when he desired to

inherit the blessing, he was rejected, for he found no

place for repentance, though he sought for it with tears.

1. Read through this passage from Hebrews 12 again and mark the following words in a distinctive way so you can spot them immediately.
     a. holiness, righteousness (Mark these two in the same way.)
     b. discipline
     c. grace

2. List everything you have learned about the discipline of the Lord from this passage. Put your information under the appropriate heading on the next page.

Who Is Disciplined?

Why Are They Disciplined?

What Is to Be the Result of Discipline?

How Are They to Respond?

What Can Happen If They Do Not Respond Properly?

Think on these things, and we will discuss them more tomorrow.

Day Six

The birthright of every child of God is grace — grace that saves, that sustains, grace that will keep you and bring you to glory. Grace eventually will produce sanctification (holiness). All of this is the birthright of those who partake of His covenant of grace.

Yet with our birthright comes responsibility. Our responsibility is that of faith. We must believe that God means what He says and stands by His Word. The grace that has brought us to salvation is sufficient to take care of our every need. We cannot say that we accept that grace and then cast it away in unbelief and return to life apart from it when the going gets rough. To do so is to despise our birthright. Apart from grace there is no hope.

Thus, the author of Hebrews illustrates what I have just said with the account of Esau from Genesis Chapters 25 and 27. When Esau came in from the fields, he was famished. "And Esau said to Jacob, 'Please let me have a swallow of that red stuff there, for I am famished.' Therefore his name was called Edom. But Jacob said, 'First sell me your birthright.' And Esau said, 'Behold, I am about to die; so of what *use* then is the birthright to me?' And Jacob said, 'First swear to me'; so he swore to him, and sold his birthright to Jacob. Then Jacob gave Esau bread and lentil stew; and he ate and drank, and rose and went on his way. Thus Esau despised his birthright" (Genesis 25:30-34).

Esau looked at the temporal — his fleshly needs — rather than at the eternal — his birthright. In the midst of a trial, he yielded to the flesh and sold his birthright for a bowl of stew! Esau reverted to the flesh. He looked at today instead of tomorrow, and he lived for today. He despised his birthright.

When we do this, we can come short of the grace of God, and as Hebrews says, a "root of bitterness" can spring up in us and defile others. Or we can become immoral or godless like Esau, who sold his birthright for a single meal (Hebrews 12:15-16).

O Beloved, you profess to know the Lord. You say that you have been saved by His grace. Beware of despising the birthright which belongs to every child of God. Realize that suffering is part of God's fatherly discipline which belongs to every child of God. He disciplines us for our good. His goal is that we become holy, or as He puts it in Hebrews, that we might share in His holiness.

Day Seven

When you suffer, remember that you have a place to run — the throne of grace. "You have not come to *a mountain* that may be touched and to a blazing fire, and to darkness and gloom and whirlwind, and to the blast of a trumpet and the sound of words which *sound was such that* those who heard begged that no further word should be spoken to them. But you have come to Mount Zion and to the city of the living God, the heavenly Jerusalem, and to myriads of angels, to the general assembly and church of the first-born who are enrolled in heaven, and to God, the Judge of all, and to the spirits of righteous men made perfect, and to Jesus, the mediator of a new covenant, and to the sprinkled blood, which speaks better than *the blood* of Abel. Therefore, since we receive a kingdom which cannot be shaken, let us show gratitude, by which we may offer to God an acceptable service with reverence and awe; for our God is a consuming fire" (Hebrews 12:18-19, 22-24, 28-29).

When you respond properly in trials, appropriating the sufficiency of His grace rather than falling short of it, the reality of the grace of God spreads, for it causes others to see in us the reality of Christ and His sufficiency. Therefore, "we have this treasure in earthen vessels, that the surpassing greatness of the power may be of God and not from ourselves; *we are* afflicted in every way, but not crushed; perplexed, but not despairing; persecuted, but not forsaken; struck down, but not destroyed; always carrying about in the body the dying of Jesus, that the life of Jesus also may be manifested in our body" (II Corinthians 4:7-10).

Have you ever seen your trials and suffering from this perspective? They are not without purpose. Nor will they destroy you. As you appropriate His all-sufficient grace, suffering and affliction become your platform for the reality of Christ. This is why Paul goes on to say, "For we who live are constantly [Did you note "constantly"?] being delivered over to death for Jesus' sake, that the life of Jesus also may be manifested in our mortal flesh. So death works in us, but life in you. For all things *are* for your sakes, that the grace which is spreading to more and more people may cause the giving of thanks to abound to the glory of God" (II Corinthians 4:11-12, 15).

Paul's sufferings were God's means of spreading His grace to others. Your suffering will do the same thing **if** you stand firm in His grace. You may not see it now, but when you stand before His throne, you will. This truth has been confirmed from one generation to another. It is recorded in the annals of church history. **When the saints suffer, it is never in vain.**

The blood of the martyrs is the seedbed of the gospel. Why? Because those without Christ realize that if they were in the Christian's shoes, they would behave differently. As we appropriate God's grace, they see us "in no way alarmed by [our] opponents — which is a sign of destruction for them, but of salvation for [us], and that *too*, from God" (Philippians 1:28).

Grace takes us **through** suffering, for we overwhelmingly conquer through Him Who loved us (Romans 8:36-37). Remember, we are afflicted, **but not crushed**; perplexed, **but not despairing**; persecuted, **but not forsaken**; struck down, **but not destroyed.** The way we suffer shows the difference between us and the lost. The difference is the grace of God — grace that not only saves us but sustains us, sufficient for every need, every trial.

Suffering is never wasted. As we share the fellowship of His sufferings, it is used to make us more like Christ and, as a result, causes the grace of God to spread, and God is glorified. Thus, Paul explains our suffering: "FOR THY SAKE WE ARE BEING PUT TO DEATH ALL DAY LONG; WE WERE CONSIDERED AS SHEEP TO BE SLAUGHTERED" (Romans 8:36). It will help to remember, my friend, that your sufferings are for His sake, endured by His grace!

I believe it will also help you to look at the Author and Finisher of your faith and remember "the grace of our Lord Jesus Christ, that though He was rich, yet for your sake He became poor, that you through His poverty might become rich" (II Corinthians 8:9). No matter what your sin, your weaknesses or inadequacies, your sufferings or the cost of Christlikeness, the grace of God has made you rich in Jesus.

Beloved reader, may "grace and peace be multiplied to you in the knowledge of God and of Jesus our Lord; seeing that His divine power has granted to us everything pertaining to life and godliness, through the true knowledge of Him who called us by His own glory and excellence. . . . Grow in the grace and knowledge of our Lord and Savior Jesus Christ" (II Peter 1:2-3; 3:18a).

"And now I commend you to God and to the word of His grace, which is able to build *you* up and to give *you* the inheritance among all those who are sanctified. To this end also [I] pray for you always that our God may count you worthy of your calling, and fulfill every desire for goodness and the work of faith with power; in order that the name of our Lord Jesus may be glorified in you, and you in Him, according to the grace of our God and the Lord Jesus Christ" (Acts 20:32; II Thessalonians 1:11-12).

Chapter 9, Notes

[1]Kellsye M. Finnie, *William Carey: By Trade a Cobbler* (Kent, England: Send the Light, 1986), p. 25.

[2]Finnie, p. 47.

[3]Finnie, p. 48.

[4]Finnie, pp. 55-57.

[5]Finnie, p. 62-65.

[6]Finnie, pp. 71-72.

[7]Finnie, p. 110.

[8]Finnie, pp. 129-130.

[9]Finnie, p. 152.

[10]Finnie, p. 151.

I pray also that the eyes of your heart may be enlightened in order that you may know the hope to which he has called you, the riches of his glorious inheritance in the saints, and his incomparably great power for us who believe.
Ephesians 1:18-19a, NIV

GROUP DISCUSSION QUESTIONS

If you want to use *Lord, I Need Grace to Make It!* as a group study, we suggest the following:

1. Prayerfully commit the study to the Lord, seeking His direction in every step.

2. Begin your first class by gathering to listen to the audio or video taped introductory lesson to *Lord, I Need Grace to Make It!* Each student should do the homework for week one before the next class. Then you would meet, have your discussion, and listen to the lecture tape for week one, etc.

3. Each student should purchase a book and do the study at home week by week.

4. After each week's lesson, have a forty- to sixty-minute class discussion. Then listen to the sixty-minute audio or video teaching tape which I have done to supplement each week's lesson. My teaching tape should always follow the class discussion, not precede it.

5. Write or call to receive information on how to order the teaching tapes and discussion leader tapes for *Lord, I Need Grace to Make It!* (These leader tapes will not be available until September, 1989. Therefore, if you have a class before then, you should develop a guide from these discussion questions. Be sure to completely review these before your class begins and be sure that you know the

answers so that you can effectively lead the discussion. Do not feel that you must use just these questions. These are a guideline to take you through the lesson and prepare you for your class.

We exist to serve you!

PRECEPT MINISTRIES
P.O. BOX 182218
CHATTANOOGA, TN 37422-7218
(615) 892-6814

WEEK ONE

1. What was the root or the basis of the sin displayed by Adam and Eve's disobedience? What is the essence of all sin?

2. When Adam and Eve were confronted with their sin, what was their response?

3. What effect did their sin have on them? What did they do? Why didn't they respond to God's call?

4. What could Adam and Eve do to redeem themselves?

5. Explain what God had said would be the consequence of disobedience on Adam and Eve's part. Did He hold the line that He had drawn against which righteousness would be measured?

6. What was God's immediate response to their sin after the consequences were realized? Did He leave them in this state?

7. What did God do to make provision for Adam and Eve? For you and me?

8. Why did God make a provision? What does this provision show us about our God?

9. We saw that grace was not seen in its fullest sense in the Old Testament. According to John 1:17, when was the grace of God truly realized?

10. Until the Son of God came, men were living under what covenant?

11. Yet how do we know that grace existed before the law? What did God do for Adam and Eve?

12. What can you and I do to earn God's grace?

13. What is the key that releases us into the grace of God?

14. Once we have believed in Jesus Christ, accepting God's provision, what can remove us from that standing or position?

15. What is the key to your relationship with your heavenly Father?

16. Which covenant do you and I live under today?

17. Explain what living under that covenant means to us in our daily lives.

18. Upon what basis does God always grant salvation?

19. After your study this week, how would you define grace? What does that mean for your life?

20. What will change in your life as a result of your study this week?

WEEK TWO

REVIEW

Last week we saw that God created man and set boundaries within which man was to live. These boundaries were not set to make man unhappy or to stifle man in any way. They were set for his good, for his protection.

We saw that man's disobedience to the standard which God had set brought death and separation from God. Then we saw how God, in His great graciousness, reached over that line and made provision for man to be reconciled to Him.

We looked at the fact that faith is the key that unlocks the grace of God. And we learned that it is by grace through faith that we are saved and that it is by grace through faith that we live a victorious Christian life day by day.

QUESTIONS

1. Why did God ever institute the old covenant?

2. What did you learn this week about the law? What was it never intended to do?

3. When the law does its job in our lives and exposes our sin, where can we turn?

4. From what you saw in the passage from Jeremiah Chapter 31, what was the main difference between the old covenant and the new covenant of which God spoke here?

5. You also read about this new covenant in a passage from Jeremiah Chapter 32. How long does the new covenant last? How do you know?

6. Once you have entered into this new covenant, will you ever turn and walk away from your God permanently? Why?

7. In Ezekiel Chapter 36, what did you learn that we are given as we enter into the new covenant?

8. What does God do that will cause us to walk in His ways?

9. As far as God is concerned, what happens to our sin when we enter into the new covenant?

10. From the passages you studied, what enables us to keep the law?

11. How do we enter into this new covenant? What is our responsibility in order to enter in? Where do we receive the ability to do that?

12. At this point, share what you see as the differences between the two covenants.

13. Upon which covenant is your daily relationship with your Father based?

14. Upon which mountain do you stand in times of failure, in times of need, in times of despair, in times of hopelessness? Why?

15. Do you see that to live under the old covenant is not to accept the graciousness of your heavenly Father Who has made a far better way for you?

16. What is your response? What will change in your life today and in the days to come as a result of the grace of God that has been poured out to all men?

WEEK THREE

REVIEW

Last week we learned that the old covenant was to serve as a schoolmaster, a tutor, to bring us to Christ. The law was to show us that we could not meet God's standard in and of ourselves.

We also learned that the new covenant would make every provision that we needed in order to live in a way that would please God. We saw that we could enter into this covenant through faith and faith alone, that we were not required to work our way into it.

We learned that upon our entry into the new covenant, God would give us new hearts, that He would write His law upon our hearts, that He would put the fear of Him on our hearts so that we would not turn away, that He would put His Spirit in us to cause us to walk in His ways, that He would supply all that we needed — it was all of grace!! We did not deserve anything because of our sin, but God in His graciousness made provision!

QUESTIONS

1. What did you see this week in Romans Chapter Three about the law?

2. How does this parallel to what you learned last week in Galatians?

3. How does the law set a standard for us and show us our need?

4. How does the law expose our sin?

5. How does the law serve as a schoolmaster, a tutor, in our lives, in the lives of our children, in the lives of our friends, etc.?

6. So often today, we hear a gospel that does not truly deal with the heart of the issue that a lost person needs to understand. What is the issue that we need to be certain they understand?

7. How is salvation often presented when someone shares the gospel? What do people often think of salvation as an escape from?

8. The lake of fire is the consequence of what?

9. What is it that we see demonstrated by God in providing a way for us to be free from the bonds of sin?

10. If we cannot keep the law, what hope do we have? How can we earn this freedom from sin?

11. What does Hebrews 2:9 say? By what did Jesus taste death for you, for me?

12. Because Jesus paid the penalty of sin, what is man able to receive?

13. In order to receive salvation and forgiveness of sin, what must man do? Can one pray to receive Christ and continue to live in the same way as before he prayed that prayer?

14. Did you receive the Holy Spirit by something that you did? How did you receive Him?

15. Our salvation then is salvation from sin. It is true that we are saved from the penalty of sin, which is the lake of fire, but what are we saved from in our daily lives as far as sin is concerned? Do we have to live in sin any longer?

16. If you are saved by grace, then what enables you to live daily over the power of sin in your life?

17. What did you see about the law that will make you more effective in sharing the gospel with your family, with those with whom you come in contact?

18. When you share the gospel, what things do you need to be certain you communicate?

19. What is the most important issue that a person must understand when they come to Jesus for salvation? How can they be set free forever?

20. How has your study of the law this week affected YOU?

Week Four

Review

Last week we studied the effect of the law in the life of an individual. We saw that the law was given to serve as a schoolmaster, a tutor, to keep us until grace would come, setting us free from the penalty and power of sin.

We saw too that man was never able, would never be able, to keep the law. And because God is gracious, He made provision for man's sin through His Son.

We again looked at the fact that it is through faith that we come to salvation, that our salvation is totally apart from the law. We saw how the law sets a righteous standard, how it reveals our sin.

We also learned that grace saves us from sin. And we talked about the fact that the lake of fire is the consequence of sin. We saw too that people are not saved from hell, but from sin.

QUESTIONS

1. What is it that will free us from our religiousness and legalism and thrust us into the freedom of a personal and intimate relationship with our heavenly Father if we will but embrace it?

2. What part does the law play in our salvation?

3. Explain how it is possible to obtain salvation through your works.

4. What is the key that unlocks the salvation of God to man? Salvation is totally apart from what?

5. Does living under the covenant of grace result in lawlessness for those who truly know Him and understand His grace?

6. What is the mark of those who live under the grace of God? What typifies their life-style?

7. Men owe God a life lived in righteousness, but man is unable to give that to God because of his own sinful

nature. What provision has God made for the man who desires to live in the way that God originally intended?

8. Is there any way that we can pay the debt we owe to God? What must we do in order to receive the gift that God has offered to us?

9. How is it possible for us to earn God's favor?

10. Explain why Christ died.

11. If we are able to be justified by the law, was there a reason for Christ to die?

12. How is your relationship with your Father begun? What is your part in your salvation? Where did you receive the ability to do what was required of you?

13. How then can your relationship be maintained?

14. Upon what basis are we ALWAYS to come to our heavenly Father?

15. At what price to our Father do you and I have access to the grace of God?

16. Explain the difference between the first Adam and the last Adam.

17. What is the limit of grace? Explain the boundary beyond which grace cannot extend.

18. Under which Adam do you live? Did you realize that there was a second Adam Who had come to set you free from the slavery under which you were born in the first Adam?

19. As you studied this week, did you see that grace, grace, grace is the key to the Christian life? Have you in some way denied the grace of God in your life? What has been your response as you have studied this lesson?

20. How has this lesson affected you? Have you ever thought that perhaps there was something in your past that was beyond the grace of God? What did you see this week that would allow you freedom from that?

21. When you see the great price paid for you to enjoy the freedom of grace, what is your response? What has changed in your heart this past week?

WEEK FIVE

REVIEW

Last week we again talked about the fact that the only basis upon which the believer could approach God was on the basis of grace.

We looked at the great price that was paid by our heavenly Father in order for our sin to be covered and for there to be a way for us to come to Him.

We saw that this price that was paid was an act of grace and that man did absolutely nothing to deserve the graciousness of God extended to him. It could not be bought by paying the debt we owed ourselves. It could not be earned through works. It could not be achieved through the keeping of the Law. It was GRACE!

And as we marveled again at the grace of God, we began to see too that it has no limits, that its capacity cannot be contained in human boundaries.

QUESTIONS

1. What is the key to being delivered from the power of sin?

2. Is it possible to live in total victory over your past, over your failures, over the pull of the flesh? How?

3. What hope do you have when you fail, when you sin?

4. Is there any relationship between grace and power? Share what your insights were as you studied and as you memorized II Corinthians 12:9-10.

5. Even though we live in the confines of a fleshly body that is weak to temptation and even though we are faced daily with the lure of the world and its enticements, what do we have available to us that will enable us to rise above the circumstances and be victorious? How is power perfected?

6. Upon what are you and I to be dependent for even our smallest daily needs, for our daily direction, for all that pertains to our daily lives?

7. What is at the root of all of our failures in the Christian life?

8. Why is it so difficult for us to accept and rely upon the grace of God?

9. How do the truths you saw in Romans 12:1-2 fit in with our study this week on grace?

10. How does having a "poor self-image" and "low self-esteem" affect your relationship with God? Is there anything that self can do that is acceptable to God?

11. From what you have studied this week, how would you define licentiousness?

12. Does the grace of God grant us the freedom to live as we please?

13. What provision has God made so that we can live under grace and yet live in a way that is pleasing to Him? (Remember your study on the new covenant.)

14. Is it possible to enter into the new covenant and then to live any way that suits you?

15. When we do fail as a Christian, is restoration possible? Why?

16. Does God ever react as man would react? God always acts from what basis?

17. Have you ever put human limitations on God? Have you thought that surely He would react in a certain way because that is how you would react? Have you released that misconception this week and stepped into the glorious liberty that is ours through grace?

18. Have you realized perhaps that there is some area in which you have taken liberty because you thought you understood the grace of God, and now you see that what you thought was liberty is really licentiousness? Have you dealt with that area and brought it under the grace of God and put it in its proper place?

19. How has this week changed your view of grace?

20. What are the things that will change in your life as a result of this week's study?

REVIEW

We learned that the key to deliverance from the power of sin is total dependence upon the grace of God in our lives.

We saw the relationship between grace and power, realizing that His grace is sufficient for every situation and that it is in our weakness that His power is perfected.

We looked at the fact that the root of all failure in the Christian life is dependence upon self. We talked about the fact that we must die to self and its ways and live in utter dependence upon grace to be what God wants us to be.

We learned that we need to be transformed by the renewing of our minds and that we are not to be conformed to the world so that we may prove the good and acceptable will of our Father.

We talked more about the fact that it is by grace and grace alone that we should live our daily lives, but we also looked at the fact that grace is never license to do as we please. We noted too that God even made provision for us to be able to walk in His grace as He gave us a new heart and placed His Spirit within us when we entered the new covenant.

QUESTIONS

1. When we run to Mt. Calvary to have our sin cleansed by the power of the blood of the Lamb, what must we do with our sin?

2. What is God's response to this action described in the previous question?

3. Once we have sinned, have run to Mt. Calvary, have been restored to fellowship, what is the next thing that we need to do? How must we look at our failure?

4. What was the promise that God made to Abram?

5. What was Sarai's response to waiting on God's perfect time to bring the promise to pass?

6. What was the result of her impatience, of her taking things into her own hands?

7. What was God's response to the situation that Sarai and Abram then found themselves in? Was God faithful to His promise?

8. What was the conflict that resulted because Sarai and Abram did not wait on God to perform His Word?

9. How does the story of Abram and Sarai in Genesis parallel the study you did in Galatians?

10. In light of your study in grace, what is the bottom-line truth that you need to learn from the story of Isaac and Ishmael?

11. What can we learn from Abraham's faith? Did he look at the circumstances or at the promise of God?

12. When you sin, what do you need to look at?

13. Is it possible to live under the covenant of grace and the covenant of the law at the same time? Under which covenant do you live?

14. Why did Christ die? Why did He set us free?

15. What is it that causes us to be "accepted in the Beloved"?

16. What must our attitude be toward sin in order for God to be able to respond in grace? What is the attitude that God must resist?

17. If one continues in willful sin, thinking that grace will cover, what has that one not understood? What was the price of grace?

18. What did you learn this week that will help you not to look at the circumstances or at your feelings when these conflict with God's Word to you?

19. The next time you sin, how are you going to deal with that sin?

20. What did you learn about pride this week? About humility?

WEEK SEVEN

REVIEW

Last week we looked at the way in which we must deal with our sin by running to the foot of the Cross for cleansing and by agreeing with God about our sin. We saw that we must call our sin "sin" and be willing to turn from it.

We studied too the story of Abraham and Sarah and the son of the free woman and the son of the bondwoman. God taught us a powerful lesson through what happened in this situation, showing us that we cannot live under two covenants — the covenant of the law and the covenant of grace. We saw too that it was the bondwoman and her son who were cast out. Again we saw in picture form that it is all of GRACE!

QUESTIONS

1. Why are we not seeing Christians having a greater impact on the world for the Kingdom of God if God truly is responsible to pour out His grace and enable them?

2. What keeps us from carrying out to its completion what God is working into our lives?

3. When we do not do what God commands or what the Word of God teaches, how does this affect the Holy Spirit?

4. How are we able to carry out to completion what God has enabled us to do? What gives us the power to be obedient?

5. Did Paul have any reason to think that he could never be used of God, that the grace of God could never cover him?

6. How did Paul overcome his past and come to the point that God could use him in the furtherance of the Kingdom?

7. How was the grace of God manifested in Paul's life?

8. Was God surprised when Paul cried out to him for salvation? Did God know who Paul was, or did God extend to Paul the grace of God and find out later that He had saved someone who had been persecuting His people?

9. Upon what basis did God save Paul?

10. Upon what basis did God save you?

11. Upon what basis are you serving God? Is it under legalism or to gain approval, or is it because of the love you have for a gracious God Who has poured out His unfathomable love toward you?

12. Did you see this week that it is by the grace of God that you are what you are? Will His grace be poured out on you in vain, or will you serve out of the obedience of love the One Who paid such a great price to offer you grace?

13. What is the most basic truth you learned this week from your study in Psalm 139?

14. Was God surprised when you came to Him? Did He have any idea about the things you had done when you were walking your own way, doing your own thing? Did He know of the ungodly things that had been done to you? Did it affect His decision to accept you in the Beloved? Why?

15. What aspect of God's character is demonstrated by the fact that He knew all about you before you ever decided to come to Him? What does this mean to you now that you know Him?

16. When things seem out of control, when you have blown it, when you have been disobedient, when you have failed miserably, do you ever want to run and hide? Does it do any good at all to try to hide from God the things that we are ashamed of, the things that we don't want anyone else to know? Why? What did you learn about His character that lets you know that you cannot hide from Him?

17. How is the particular attribute of God described on the previous page a comfort to you as His child?

18. Are you ever unhappy with the way you look, with your height, with your weight, with the length of your nose, with the size of your feet, with the color of your hair, etc.? Who made you? How do you know that He made you just the way He wanted you to be to bring Him the most glory?

19. Sometimes do you wonder how you will make it? Who is the One Who will sustain you?

20. Has someone wronged you? Do you wonder how you will be vindicated? What did you see about your God this week that allows you to rest in Him regarding this concern?

WEEK EIGHT

REVIEW

We talked about the fact that it may appear to be a contradiction when we talk about the grace of God being available for every situation and then we look at some Christians who do not seem to be as effective as others. When we look at the state of Christendom, we may wonder why the Kingdom of God does not progress more expediently. We looked at Scriptures that helped us to understand that we are the bottleneck, that we need to work out our salvation.

We looked at the way Paul responded to the grace of God in his life, and we discussed the fact that he could have let his past overcome him had he not understood and appropriated the grace of God.

Then finally we looked at Psalm 139 to get a perspective on our God and His understanding of us, and we came to an even better understanding of His graciousness toward us through this study.

QUESTIONS

1. What is the obligation that grace carries with it?

2. How are we able to fulfill this obligation?

3. What gives us access to the grace of God?

4. What does it mean to have access to the grace of God? How will this understanding affect you moment by moment?

5. When would God's grace be poured out on you in vain?

6. In His grace, with what has God provided you so that you can serve the Body of Jesus Christ?

7. What purpose do the gifts serve?

8. Are all of these gifts alike? Do they all have the same result?

9. How is it determined which gift(s) you will receive? When do you receive the gift(s)?

10. In your study this week, what did you learn about the purpose of your life?

11. Will you be able to serve God no matter what He brings into your life? Why? Share the example of this from Paul's life.

12. We all have access to the grace of God, but what activates the grace of God?

13. By what are we able to unlock all of the resources of God which He has made available to us?

14. Grace strips us of everything except what?

15. What gives faith its strength?

16. What is necessary in order to lay hold of grace?

17. If you do not appropriate the grace of God, how can this affect your service for Him?

18. What did you learn this week about grace and faith that will change your perspective forever?

19. What is your spiritual gift which you have been given to serve the Body? What is the ministry in which you use your gift? (Do not feel badly if you do not know; just determine before God to find out by studying His Word and by waiting on Him to show you.)

WEEK NINE

REVIEW

Last week our study centered on the fact that grace carries with it the obligation to use to the fullest extent possible the grace of God poured out in your life.

We looked again at the fact that the grace of God is activated and appropriated by faith. We saw too that our faith is as strong as the object in which we have placed it.

A new insight that we gained last week was that we have each been given a spiritual gift(s) by which to serve the Body. We saw that by using this gift we were appropriating the grace of God through faith in service to our brothers and sisters.

We talked too about the fact that grace could be poured out on us in vain, and we talked about how to be certain that this would not be the case in our lives.

QUESTIONS

1. What did you learn about grace from the passage in II Corinthians 12 that you studied this week?

2. Are we to never suffer trials, sufferings, heartaches because we belong to the Lord?

3. If trials do come, what assurance do we have in the midst of them?

4. Does God ever place us in a trial or into a time of suffering that we are not able to handle? How do you know?

5. What does the Scripture mean when it says that God will provide the way of escape in any temptation?

6. Can you explain the sufficiency of His grace for every trial of life? How is His grace sufficient?

7. What purpose do trials serve in our lives?

8. Again, you saw the relationship between power and grace. Can you explain it? What does that mean for you?

9. From what you saw this week in Hebrews, why are we disciplined?

10. What is the result of the discipline of the Lord?

11. In the discipline process, what is our responsibility?

12. What can happen in the midst of a trial if we do not respond properly?

13. Grace is a free gift of God to His children. But what is our responsibility regarding grace?

14. What was Esau's mistake in his trial? What lesson can we learn from the way he responded?

15. Where are we to run when we find ourselves in the midst of a trial?

16. When we respond properly in a trial, what effect does it have on others?

17. What will carry us through the trial, the suffering?

18. How will you respond the next time you find yourself in the midst of a trial, in suffering?

19. As you enter into a trial, what verse do you need to remember and keep ever before you?

20. What have you learned this week about the discipline of the Lord?